EDITED BY **JAMES MURPHY**

SERIES EDITOR **TOM BENNETT**

THE research **ED** GUIDE TO

LITERACY

....

AN EVIDENCE-INFORMED
GUIDE FOR TEACHERS

First Published 2019

by John Catt Educational Ltd,
15 Riduna Park, Station Road,
Melton, Woodbridge IP12 1QT

Tel: +44 (0) 1394 389850
Email: enquiries@johncatt.com
Website: www.johncatt.com

© **John Catt Educational**

ISBN: 978 1 912906 42 0

Set and designed by John Catt Educational Limited

WHAT IS researchED?

researchED is an international, grassroots education-improvement movement that was founded in 2013 by Tom Bennett, a London-based high school teacher and author. researchED is a truly unique, teacher-led phenomenon, bringing people from all areas of education together onto a level playing field. Speakers include teachers, principals, professor, researchers and policy makers.

Since our first sell-out event, researchED has spread all across the UK, into the Netherlands, Norway, Sweden, Australia, the USA, with events planned in Spain, Japan, South Africa and more. We hold general days as well as themed events, such as researchED Maths & Science, or researchED Tech.

WHO ARE WE?

Since 2013, researchED has grown from a tweet to an international conference movement that so far has spanned six continents and thirteen countries. We have simple aims: to help teaching become more evidence-facing; to raise the research literacy in teaching; to improve education research standards; and to bring research users and research creators closer together. To do this, we hold unique one-day conferences that bring together teachers, researchers, academics and anyone touched by research. We believe in teacher voice, and short-circuiting the top-down approach to education that benefits no one.

HOW DOES IT WORK?

The gathering of mainly teachers, researchers, school leaders, policymakers and edu-bloggers creates a unique dynamic. Teachers and researchers can attend the sessions all day and engage with each other to exchange ideas. The vast majority of speakers stay for the duration of the conference, visit each other's sessions, work on the expansion of their knowledge and gain a deeper understanding of the work of their peers. Teachers can take note of recent developments in educational research, but are also given the opportunity to provide feedback on the applicability of research or practical obstacles.

CONTENTS

FOREWORD

BY TOM BENNETT

Nowhere in education is the gap between the intuitive and the evidence-informed approach greater than in the discussion, practice and implementation of teaching children how to be literate. And nowhere is the need to separate the former from the latter more urgent. There can be no more pressing of an issue for a child's education than to enable them to be able to read and learn independently from the written records of others, and the ability for them to record their own thoughts, observations and contributions to the great rolling ocean of human culture and wisdom.

Without this faculty, we condemn children to a solipsistic existence where memory is the only reservoir of one's knowledge, and voice our only medium with which to interrogate, communicate or express it. Reading and writing are often claimed to be our greatest inventions as a species, representative of our earliest and most profound accomplishments. This might be because of the liberation it affords us, both individually and as a species. Suddenly we become free from merely oral traditions, extraordinary as they are, and gain the ability to accumulate experience, to build upon the countless lives of others and their thoughts because they have been codified and shared. Our global evolution has been facilitated and accelerated by the act of carving and recording symbols on clay, papyrus and screen.

Consider the life of a child denied this inheritance. No child is born with this faculty; unlike verbal language it must be instructed. In E. R. Burroughs' fantasy story *Tarzan*, the eponymous hero teaches himself to read (but not speak) by studying early reading primers in his dead parent's cabin. But this capacity is as improbable as his physical acumen. For all but fictional characters, reading is a gift given to us by our elders.

For too many children, this is a gift imperfectly given. We celebrate literacy rates in the wealthiest of countries, but ignore the fact that all children are capable of being literate, in the absence of a cognitive or neurological impairment. One child leaving their early education functionally illiterate, or reading well below their average age capacity is one too many. For every child who leaves formal education in this unhappy state we should ask 'Why?'

And yet the evidence bases available to us in the fields of reading instruction are among the most robust of any fields in education. We still see too many children failing to acquire the skills they need to flourish, not for want of investment or time in their education, but in the imperfect understanding of their instructors of how best to teach children to read and write. The reasons for this are historical, ideological, tribal and all too human. They are the same reasons some cling to homeopathy, swear by witchcraft, or refuse to believe smoking increases their risk of cancer: superstition, faith over facts, emotional approaches to empirical science, cultural affection, and every frailty of reason imaginable.

No more. Enough. *Enough*. Throughout the world, children – and adults – groan under the burden of illiteracy. And it is an entirely unnecessary burden. Evidence bases abound to demonstrate this. And this book, ably compiled and edited by one of its best guides and interpreters, James Murphy, is – I hope – a contribution to the effort to build a world where no student leaves school illiterate, and every human that draws breath can read every brilliant thought that has ever been expressed, and write better ones. I started researchED for exactly this kind of reason, and I hope this book begins conversations and discussions that take seed, root and blossom in the minds of children everywhere.

INTRODUCTION

BY JAMES MURPHY

What do we mean by literacy?

Every domain of knowledge has a literacy handle these days, it seems: there is digital literacy, cultural literacy, critical literacy, emotional literacy, financial literacy… the list is very long. The appropriation of the term to these other domains has somewhat diminished the power of the original term, in much the same way that clichés lose their original meaning. But what all these terms have in common is that the 'literacy' part denotes mastery of the conventions of that domain. Digital literacy means that we are familiar enough with how computers work to be able to use them to process information; financial literacy means that we know the basics about how to manage our money, so that we don't get caught out by deals that sound good but aren't. In the same way, literacy in its original sense means mastery of the written code (the spoken language represented by 'letters', hence 'literacy'). It is shallow thinking to conceive of such vital skills as 'basic' or 'lower order'; in our modern world, they are the intellectual equivalent of breathing. Do you regard breathing as 'lower order', or as essential?

Reading and writing are such ubiquitous activities, that we perform so effortlessly, that we are often barely conscious of the action. This knowledge did not evolve biologically – reading and writing are human inventions, about 4000 years old, that have transformed our ability to record, store and transmit language across time and distance. As a result, they have enabled successive generations to build on the learning of those who have gone before. They have enabled the accumulation of that vast body of cultural artefacts that we call literature – recording voices, perspectives and experiences that could only be recorded because the authors knew the secret of how to write; and that we can only access because we know the secret of how to read. They have enabled participation in political and social discourse in a way that would have been regarded as impossible even 150 years ago. Written language has become the foundation on which the information revolution is built. Without access to this foundation, full participation in our society is impossible. Indeed, poor literacy is so strongly correlated with poor life outcomes that it should be impossible to ignore. Yet there is strong evidence that education systems around the world are perpetuating social inequality by systematically producing about one-fifth of school leavers who are functionally illiterate.

To turn this situation around, we need to ensure that everyone involved in education is free of the many myths and fads that have bedevilled our teaching practice; that the widespread apathy around reversing illiteracy is banished; and that teachers understand both the 'what' and the 'how' of developing strong literacy skills for all students.

In the chapters that follow, an international cast of professionals from both research and practice backgrounds sets about this task. This book is for every teacher who wants to lay the foundations of good literacy practice. We begin with Professor Kathleen Rastle tracing the journey towards skilled reading, and continue with Dr Kerry Hempenstall making the case for evidence-based practice, dispelling many of the myths and misconceptions that have been substitutes for such practice. Dr Jessie Ricketts and James Murphy consider the essentials of literacy assessment, what schools can do to get it right and why it is so important. Professor Kevin Wheldall, Dr Robyn Wheldall, and Dr Jennifer Buckingham join forces to explain how early intervention with literacy problems at primary school can solve problems that many would have us believe are irremediable. Professor Rhona Stainthorp outlines what research tells us about the effective teaching of spelling, Tom Needham describes how vital writing skills can be communicated, and Alex Quigley summarises the research on the explicit teaching of vocabulary. Lastly, Dianne Murphy makes the case that even at secondary school, effective literacy intervention can make a massive difference to students' lives.

This book is not intended to be the last word on reading and writing. That task is quite probably impossible. We would, however, be very happy if it became the first word on the subject: if it spared thousands of teachers the painful journey to discovering that what they have been told about reading and writing is mere folklore; and if millions more children were taught well the first time around, so that school became a place, not of stress and humiliation, but of security and success.

The journey starts here: please, join us.

THE JOURNEY TO SKILLED READING

BY KATHLEEN RASTLE

For most of us, reading seems as effortless and natural as breathing. It seems a puzzle, therefore, that reading is the most researched topic in education, and that there is still much about the cognitive processes involved in reading that is not yet clear. What we do know, however, is agreed upon by an unusually strong consensus across the scientific community, and what this community has learnt in the last 40 years has forever altered our understanding and beliefs about reading, literacy and even human intelligence.

Unfortunately, and mysteriously, this knowledge has not transferred to the community of teaching practitioners; indeed, it has consistently been challenged, resisted and attacked. As a result, teachers and children have missed out, with direct, painful and costly consequences for society. In this chapter, Professor Kathleen Rastle elegantly pulls together the vast body of research on this topic into a coherent, thoughtful and balanced analysis. Make no mistake: every teacher, regardless of their subject specialism, should be familiar with the story that follows.

Author bio-sketch:

Kathleen Rastle is Professor of Cognitive Psychology at Royal Holloway, University of London. Her research is focused on reading acquisition, skilled reading, and their relationship to spoken language. She has a particular interest in understanding how properties of human learning impact on the acquisition of reading skill. Rastle's research has been reported on television, radio and in print media, and her research has influenced policy and practice in the area of literacy. She has a keen interest in making research accessible to teachers, helping to make sure that research findings are translated to successful classroom practices for the benefit of all children. Rastle is the Editor in Chief for the Journal of Memory and Language and serves in senior positions in the Economic and Social Research Council. She is a Fellow of the Academia Europaea and the Academy of Social Sciences of the United Kingdom.

Learning to read is the most important milestone of a child's education. Reading unlocks knowledge, work, social interaction and public services. But reading also transforms human capability, because it allows us to access language through vision – to experience 'language at the speed of sight'.[1] Virtually all purposeful activity in modern society involves interaction with text. Thus, it is hard to conceive of any 21st century skill that is more important than skilled reading. Yet, large-scale studies routinely show that a large percentage of children reach the end of formal schooling without the baseline reading skills to participate fully in life.[2]

The ubiquity of reading in modern society contrasts with the fact that reading is a relatively recent cultural invention. The earliest writing systems began to emerge only around 5000 years ago, and the phenomenon of mass public literacy that we know today has developed in the timescale of generations. This disconnect between the speed of human evolution and the cultural evolution of reading reminds us that children do not have an inborn capacity for reading. Though most children will learn to speak and understand simply through experience with spoken language, learning to read is a painstaking process requiring reconfiguration of neural systems,[3] based on years of instruction, dedication and practice.

Skill acquisition versus skilled behaviour

Reading and reading acquisition have been very well studied in the psychological sciences, but translation from research to practice has been slow and often marred by ideological debate. One of the reasons why translation has been difficult is the sheer complexity of reading. Though understanding the following sentence seems effortless to a skilled adult reader, it involves a myriad of mental processes:[4]
'Jess decided to cut and run – she couldn't face what might happen next.'

Visual processes include analysis of the lines, curves and dots that make up letters in the words. This task is not at all straightforward, as the letters of the Roman alphabet comprise a highly confusable matrix, in which small visual differences in shape (e.g. *cut* versus *cub*) or position (e.g. *run* versus *urn*) yield large differences in meaning. The comprehension of sentences depends on understanding individual words, but note that the words in the sentence above are sometimes ambiguous (e.g. *face*), or are used in a figurative manner (e.g. *cut and run*). The reader might also be using background knowledge and inferencing skills to determine what might have perpetuated Jess's predicament.[4] Finally, these processes arise within a highly-sophisticated eye-movement system, tuned over many years to facilitate rapid text comprehension.[5]

Knowing all that reading involves, it is not surprising that there has been such intense debate over how to teach children to read. If reading is about deriving nuanced shades of meaning from a text, then why should initial reading instruction focus on phonics, for example?

It is useful to consider an analogy here to another skilled behaviour – mountain biking. Hurtling down a steep and rocky course on a mountain bike requires rapid decisions and refinements related to balance, pressure, steering and braking that are learnt over many years. But it seems obvious that one would never teach all of these skills to a child learning to ride a bike for the first time. Instead, the use of stabilisers allows the child to gain competence in basic skills (e.g. steering and pedaling) that will later support mastery of the tricky problem of balance. Likewise, initial reading instruction is intended to provide the support system for children to build basic word recognition skills that will be essential for the development of higher-level text comprehension.

Learning to decode single words

Learning to read begins with spoken language. Substantial evidence suggests that vocabulary, grammar and narrative ability prior to reading acquisition predict later reading comprehension ability.[6] Likewise, research suggests that interventions on oral language have impacts on later reading comprehension.[7] Finally, while most children begin school with a good foundation of oral language, a recent population study suggests that up to two children in every classroom may have impaired language.[8] These data suggest that low language in the early years is an important risk factor for later reading difficulty.

Though spoken language skills are an important foundation for reading, these skills are not sufficient on their own to support reading acquisition. Instead, children require additional instruction to learn to map the visual symbols that make up printed words onto oral language knowledge. Figure 1 on the next page illustrates two ways in which this might be achieved.

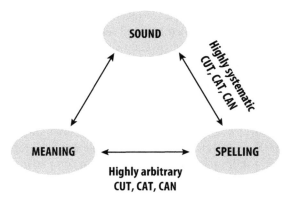

Figure 1. Dual pathways to meaning. The pathway between spelling and sound is largely systematic, but the pathway between spelling and meaning is largely arbitrary for simple words.

One possibility might be to map printed words onto meanings directly. However, for the short words that comprise most of a child's initial year of reading instruction, this mapping between spelling and meaning is arbitrary. Though the words *cut, cat* and *can* look similar, for example, these words are not similar in meaning. The lack of any regularity here means that these words would need to be memorised one by one; nothing about learning one word would assist learning of another. This type of rote learning is very challenging, and would be simply unfeasible for a language like English characterised by such a large vocabulary. Indeed, while mastery of around 4000 characters is considered sufficient for full literacy in Chinese, the average English reader is able to recognise around 70,000 printed words by the time they are 20.[4]

The other possibility is to map printed words onto sounds and compute meaning via oral language knowledge. Learning along the print-to-sound pathway is highly systematic. For example, the words *cut, cat* and *can* look similar and also sound similar. Consequently, learning one of these words will assist learning of another, and indeed other new words comprising the same spelling-sound combinations (e.g. *nut*). Alphabetic writing systems vary in the regularity of the spelling-to-sound relationship; for example, printed Italian words are relatively straightforward to pronounce by rule, whereas English is characterised by a relatively high degree of irregularity (e.g. *pint* versus *mint, hint* and *lint*; *have* versus *save, gave* and *wave*). However, though around 19% of English words have some irregularity, typically this is restricted to a single symbol-sound association within these words, with all other associations consistent with a relatively simple set of rules. Thus, even in English, this mapping is still considered to be highly systematic.[4]

Systematic learning is far less challenging than arbitrary learning, and that is why researchers recommend focusing initial reading instruction on the spelling-to-sound relationship as a pathway to meaning. However, though this mapping is systematic, the notion that discrete visual units represent a continuous speech stream is profound and non-intuitive. Indeed, though it is often thought that this insight will come naturally through experience with text (e.g. through shared storybook reading) this is not supported by the evidence.[4,9] Rather, research suggests that most children require explicit instruction in order to appreciate how visual symbols relate to spoken language. The purpose of systematic phonics is to provide this instruction.[4]

Systematic phonics instruction

Decades of research have shown that appreciating the spelling-sound relationship is a necessary foundation of reading, and that systematic phonics instruction is the most effective way of helping a child to acquire this foundation.[4] Systematic phonics is method of instruction whereby the sounds of spoken language (phonemes) are linked explicitly to the visual symbols (graphemes) that represent them. For example, a child may be taught that the graphemes <f>, <ph> and <ff> all map to the sound /f/; they may also be taught how to blend the sound /f/ with the other sounds in a word (e.g. <fun> = /f/ /V/ /n/, /fVn/).

Relevant research findings have been synthesised through several national inquiries, all of which have recommended use of systematic phonics in initial reading instruction.[10, 11] However, though the first of these major reviews was published 20 years ago, high-quality phonics instruction is still lacking in many classrooms. Further, even where some phonics provision is present, this is often an unstructured part of a 'balanced literacy' or 'multi-cuing' programme that encourages guessing from context or pictures. These approaches are ineffective and therefore waste valuable teaching time. More importantly, they may actually cause harm because they provide children with strategies to avoid learning the spelling-to-sound relationship.[12] Unfortunately, these strategies will fail as text becomes more difficult.

The provision of systematic phonics instruction has been a legal requirement in state primary schools in England for over ten years. This policy developed further in 2012 with the introduction of a phonics screen conducted toward the end of Year 1 (when children are five or six years old). The phonics screen requires children to read aloud 20 simple words and 20 simple non-words (e.g. *bim, thazz*). Non-words are the most important part of this screen because they provide a pure measure of spelling-sound knowledge – they cannot be read aloud based on memory for individual words. If children do not reach a good standard in the phonics screen, they receive additional instruction and are retested at the end of Year 2. Figure 2 below presents data from each year of the phonics screen.

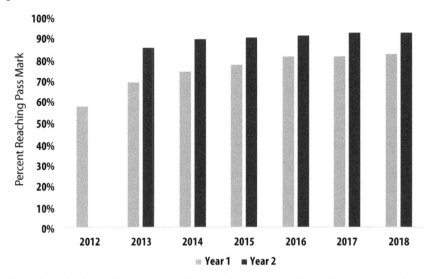

Figure 2. Results of the phonics screen in England. Bars show the percentage of children reaching the pass mark when tested at the end of Year 1, and then following the Year 2 retest for those children who did not pass on the first occasion.

One notable feature of these data is that only 58% of children reached a satisfactory standard the first year that it was introduced. This figure is important because it came five years after publication of 'Letters and Sounds', a substantial government document provided to all primary schools describing the principles and practice of high-quality phonics instruction.[13] These data suggests that it is not enough to recommend that systematic phonics should be provided or even to require it. Schools must have the means to test the effectiveness of their own practice. Indeed, an evaluation of the phonics screen in 2015 provided evidence that schools had changed their practice each year on the basis of the screening results.[14] The other notable feature of these data is the dramatic, year-on-year improvement since introduction of the phonics screen, reflecting tens of thousands of additional children each year developing the foundations to become skilled readers. Research on phonics screen performance suggests that it measures what it is supposed to measure and that it is sufficiently sensitive to identify at-risk readers.[15] There is no evidence that strong readers are disadvantaged by being asked to read non-words.[15, 16]

Building fluency through orthographic learning

Longitudinal research suggests that virtually all of the variation in reading ability at the age of seven is explained by spoken language ability and decoding ability.[17] Substantial evidence suggests that knowledge of the spelling-sound relationship continues to support skilled, adult reading. This type of knowledge is essential when encountering unfamiliar words (e.g. *blog, tweet*), but we also know that sound-based codes are computed as a matter of routine in skilled reading. It is for this reason that we are able to understand phrases like '*dog will bight*'. Evidence suggests that these computations are relatively rapid, and arise in text reading even before a word is fixated (i.e. when words are in the periphery).[18] However, models of skilled reading agree that spelling-sound knowledge on its own is insufficient to drive rapid, skilled reading, and that ultimately a direct mapping between printed words and their meanings is required.[19, 20]

Much less is known about how this mapping is acquired (as opposed to the spelling-sound mapping). Evidence from neuroscience suggests that it involves a repurposing of the brain regions built for object and face recognition, so that neurons in those regions become tuned to orthographic stimuli.[3] Further, longitudinal work suggests that the sensitivity of these regions to printed words continues to change at least into adolescence.[21] These data highlight the fact that stored knowledge about the meanings of printed words arises gradually as a result of text experience over many years. This process is sometimes referred to as 'orthographic learning'.[22]

The most prominent theory of orthographic learning suggests that it arises through an accumulation of text experience, as a child uses their spelling-sound knowledge as a *self-teaching* device.[23] On Share's self-teaching theory,[23] when a reader repeatedly decodes an unfamiliar word into a known spoken language representation, then that results in the acquisition of an orthographic representation for that word. Critically, that orthographic representation can be recognised without translation to a sound-based code. In this way, though reading increasingly relies on a direct mapping between spelling and meaning, phonic knowledge acts as the stabilisers (thinking back to our cycling analogy) in bringing the child to that point.

It is widely accepted that beyond oral language and systematic phonics instruction, the most important ingredient of skilled reading is text experience.[24] Text experience varies widely, and there is very substantial variation in the number of printed words that adult readers report having encountered.[25] It is often argued that systematic phonics instruction may turn children off learning to read for pleasure, but to my knowledge there is no evidence for this view.

Rather, systematic phonics instruction provides the foundational skills needed in order to begin to read independently, and thus build the vital text experience necessary to become a skilled reader.[4] Recent behaviour-genetic modelling supports this claim by finding a causal relationship between reading well and reading often (i.e. reading well permits reading often, rather than the reverse).[26] In short, there is no opposition between systematic phonics instruction and reading for pleasure. Reading for pleasure is vitally important, and phonic knowledge enables this, rather than prevents it.

It is important to consider what children are learning through all of this text experience. Certainly, they are learning about the function, meaning and frequency of individual words. But they are also learning about the morphological structure of the language and writing system. The vast majority of English words are built from stems (e.g. *book*) combined with other stems (e.g. *book*worm), or affixes (e.g. *book*ish). This morphological structure turns out to be important for learning the direct spelling-meaning mapping because this is an area of non-arbitrariness within that mapping. This is because stems occur and reoccur with highly similar meanings (e.g. un*clean*, *clean*er, *clean*ly, *clean*liness), and affixes alter the meanings of stems in highly predictable ways (e.g. teach*er*, build*er*, bank*er*). If a child understands the morphological structure of the writing system, then the task of orthographic learning becomes much simpler. For example, the words un*clean*, *clean*er, *clean*ly and *clean*liness all become variations of a single word. Estimates suggest that this knowledge reduces the orthographic learning challenge around seven-fold, to learning around 11,000 stems on average.[27, 28]

Morphology provides highly salient information regarding the likely meaning of a word, and accounts for much of the spelling-sound inconsistency of English. Research suggests that skilled, adult readers analyse this information in the first 200m/s of the recognition process, and that sensitivity to this information is related to the structure of the direct spelling-meaning brain pathway.[28] In view of the importance of morphology in the writing system, it is likely that children would benefit from morphological instruction at some point in the acquisition process. However, there is insufficient evidence to recommend when that instruction should take place and what form it should take. Only systematic phonics instruction can assist children to learn the 11,000 or so stems at the foundation of the English vocabulary.[27]

Text comprehension and impacts on spoken language

The purpose of learning to read is not to recognise individual words but to engage with text. However, understanding of phrases and sentences is built from knowledge of the meanings of individual words, and an important reason for poor reading comprehension is poor reading at the level of single words. Further, if a child is able to recognise individual words rapidly, they are able to turn limited-capacity working memory resources to the problem of higher-level comprehension.

Understanding text relies on spoken language ability. However, recent corpus-based research suggests that text tends to use higher-level vocabulary and more complex syntax than spoken language.[29] This is immediately apparent in the following sentence of Jack London's *The Call of the Wild*, a popular book for children in Key Stage 3 of England's National Curriculum (pupils between the ages of 11 and 14):

> Deep in the forest a call was sounding, and as often as he heard this call, mysteriously thrilling and luring, he felt compelled to turn his back upon the fire and the beaten earth around it, and to plunge into the forest, and on and on, he knew not where or why; nor did he wonder where or why, the call sounding imperiously, deep in the forest.

London's passage gives us pause to consider how text experience shapes overall language knowledge. It is widely thought that reading to children conveys important language benefits, even if it does not provide a mechanism to acquire the print skills necessary for reading.[9] The fact that text comprises more sophisticated vocabulary than matched child-directed speech provides one way in which these language benefits might arise (i.e. by exposing children to a wider range of language input).[29] It may be possible for these benefits to continue into secondary school, particularly if the text being read to children is more difficult than they are reading independently. It is also clear that text experience gained through independent reading provides a critical source of language knowledge. Indeed, research suggests that children and adults acquire knowledge of complex syntactic structures (e.g. relative clauses and passives) through their experience with text and use these structures in their own spoken language production.[30]

More generally, while there is broad consensus that spoken language provides the foundation for reading acquisition, an emerging body of literature suggests that there may be reciprocal benefits of literacy on spoken language. The acquisition of literacy is thought to facilitate spoken word learning, sharpen phonological representations, enhance phonological awareness (the ability to manipulate spoken input) and improve predictive ability.[31, 32] So, learning to read may provide an important mechanism to address the variability in spoken language ability in young children thought to contribute to the achievement gap as schooling progresses.

Concluding remarks

It is difficult to imagine a life without reading and all that flows from learning to read. But over 15% of children leave school without the baseline literacy skills to participate fully in society.[2] Those children will become adults with severely limited opportunities, who are potentially unable to transmit positive literacy behaviours to their own children.[33] The direct and indirect impacts, the lost opportunities, and the intergenerational aspects of low literacy surely mean that there is no more important function of compulsory education than to teach children to read. We have a short space of time during the school years in which to achieve this, and it is therefore imperative that the most effective instructional methods are used. Fortunately, 50 years of research has allowed us to develop a good understanding of the process of reading acquisition. It is now up to scientists, teachers, SENCOs, literacy specialists, school leaders and government to work together to implement best practice based on this research for the benefit of all children.

References

The issues considered in this brief article are considered much more deeply in: Castles, A., Rastle, K., and Nation, K. (2018) 'Ending the reading wars: Reading acquisition from novice to expert', *Psychological Science in the Public Interest* 9 pp. 5-51. This substantial open access article synthesises the most important findings from the past 50 years of reading research (citing over 350 original articles), and considers their implications for classroom practice. Sources for the arguments made in this article are included below for completeness.

1. Seidenberg, M. (2017) *Language at the speed of sight: How we read, why so many can't, and what can be done about it.* New York, NY: Basic Books.

2. Organisation for Economic Cooperation and Development (2016) *Programme for international student assessment results from PISA 2015: United Kingdom.* Retrieved from: www.bit.ly/2osoUOU

3. Dehaene, S. and Cohen, L. (2011) 'The unique role of the visual word form area in reading', *Trends in Cognitive Sciences* 15 (6) pp. 254-262.

4. Castles, A., Rastle, K. and Nation, K. (2018) 'Ending the reading wars: Reading acquisition from novice to expert', *Psychological Science in the Public Interest* 19 (1) pp. 5-51.

5. Rayner, K. (2009) 'Eye movements and attention in reading, scene perception, and visual search', *Quarterly Journal of Experimental Psychology* 62 (8) pp. 1457-1506.

6. Nation, K., Cocksey, J., Taylor, J. S. and Bishop, D. V. (2010) 'A longitudinal investigation of early reading and language skills in children with poor reading comprehension', *Journal of Child Psychology and Psychiatry* 51 (9) pp. 1031-1039.

7. Clarke, P. J., Snowling, M. J., Truelove, E. and Hulme, C. (2010) 'Ameliorating children's reading-comprehension difficulties: A randomized controlled trial', *Psychological Science* 21 (8) pp. 1106-1116.

8. Norbury, C. F., Gooch, D., Wray, C., Baird, G., Charman, T., Simonoff, E., Vamvakas, G. and Pickles, A. (2016) 'The impact of nonverbal ability on prevalence and clinical presentation of language disorder: evidence from a population study', *Journal of Child Psychology and Psychiatry* 57 (11) pp. 1247-1257.

9. Treiman, R. (2018) 'What research tells us about reading instruction', *Psychological Science in the Public Interest* 19 (1) pp. 1-4.

10. Ehri, L. C., Nunes, S. R., Stahl, S. A. and Willows, D. M. (2001) 'Systematic phonics instruction helps students learn to read: Evidence from the National Reading Panel's meta-analysis', *Review of Educational Research* 71 (3) pp. 393-447.

11. Rose, J. (2006) *Independent review of the teaching of early reading final report.* Retrieved from: www.bit.ly/1MkcXOf

12. Landi, N., Perfetti C. A., Bolger, D. J., Dunlap, S. and Foorman, B. R. (2006) 'The role of discourse context in developing word form representations: A paradoxical relation between reading and learning', *Journal of Experimental Child Psychology* 94 (2) pp. 114-133.

13. Department for Education and Skills (2007) *Letters and sounds: Principles and practice of high-quality phonics.* London: The Stationery Office.

14. Walker, M., Sainsbury, M., Worth, J., Bamforth, H. and Betts, H. (2015) *Phonics screening check evaluation: Final report.* Retrieved from: www.bit.ly/2nIYbNU

15. Duff, F. J., Mengoni, S. E., Bailey. A. M. and Snowling, M. J. (2014) 'Validity and sensitivity of the phonics screening check: implications for practice', *Journal of Research in Reading* 38 (2) pp. 109-123.

16. Castles, A., Polito, V., Pritchard, S., Anandakumar, T. and Coltheart, M. (2018) 'Do nonword reading tests for children measure what we want them to? An analysis of year 2 error responses', *Australian Journal of Learning Difficulties* 23 (2) pp. 153-165.

17. Hjetland, H. N., Lervåg, A., Lyster, S. A. H., Hagtvet, B. E., Hulme, C. and Melby-Lervåg, M. (2019) 'Pathways to reading comprehension: A longitudinal study from 4 to 9 years of age', *Journal of Educational Psychology* 111 (5) pp. 751-763.

18. Leineger, M. (2014) 'Phonological coding during reading', *Psychological Bulletin* 140 (6) pp. 1534-1555.

19. Harm, M. W. and Seidenberg, M. S. (2004) 'Computing the meanings of words in reading: Cooperative division of labor between visual and phonological processes', *Psychological Review* 111 (3) pp. 662-720.

20. Coltheart, M., Rastle, K., Perry, C., Langdon, R. and Ziegler, J. (2001) 'DRC: A dual route cascaded model of visual word recognition and reading aloud', *Psychological Review* 108 (1) pp. 204-256.

21. Ben-Shachar, M., Dougherty, R. F., Deutsch, G. K. and Wandell, B. A. (2011) 'The development of cortical sensitivity to visual word forms', *Journal of Cognitive Neuroscience* 23 (9) pp. 2387-2399.

22. Castles, A. and Nation, K. (2006) 'How does orthographic learning happen?' in Andrews, S. (Ed.) *From inkmarks to ideas: Current issues in lexical processing.* Hove: Psychology Press, pp. 151-179.

23. Share, D. L. (1995) 'Phonological recoding and self-teaching: Sine qua non of reading acquisition', *Cognition* 55 (2) pp. 151-218.

24. Nation, K. (2017) 'Nurturing a lexical legacy: Reading experience is critical for the development of word reading skill', *Npj Science of Learning* 2 (3) pp. 1-4.

25. Brysbaert, M., Stevens, M., Mandera, P. and Keuleers, E. (2016) 'How many words do we know? Practical estimates of vocabulary size dependent on word definition, the degree of language input and the participant's age', *Frontiers in Psychology* 29 (7) p. 1116.

26. Bergen, E., Snowling, M. J., Zeeuw, E. L., Beijsterveldt, C. E., Dolan, C. V. and Boomsma, D. I. (2018) 'Why do children read more? The influence of reading ability on voluntary reading practices', *Journal of Child Psychology and Psychiatry* 59 (11) pp. 1205-1214.

27. Rastle, K. (2019) 'The place of morphology in learning to read in English', *Cortex* 116 pp. 45-54.

28. Rastle, K. (2019) 'EPS mid-career prize lecture 2017: Writing systems, reading, and language', *Quarterly Journal of Experimental Psychology* 72 (4) pp. 677-692.

29. Montag, J. L., Jones, M. N. and Smith, L. B. (2015). 'The words children hear: Picture books and the statistics for language learning', *Psychological Science* 26 (9) pp. 1489-1496.

30. Montag, J. L. and MacDonald, M. C. (2015) 'Text exposure predicts spoken production of complex sentences in 8-and 12-year-old children and adults', *Journal of Experimental Psychology: General* 144 (2) pp. 447-468.

31. Castles, A. and Coltheart, M. (2004) 'Is there a causal link from phonological awareness to success in learning to read?', *Cognition* 91 (1) pp. 77-111.

32. Huettig, F. and Pickering, M. J. (2019) 'Literacy advantages beyond reading: Prediction of spoken language', *Trends in Cognitive Sciences* 23 (6) pp. 464-475.

33. Bergen, E., Zuijen, T., Bishop, D. and Jong, P. F. (2017) 'Why are home literacy environment and children's reading skills associated? What parental skills reveal', *Reading Research Quarterly* 52 (2) pp. 147-160.

MYTHS AND EVIDENCE

BY KERRY HEMPENSTALL

Throughout recent decades, education has been plagued by myths and what Professor Graham Nuthall termed the 'folklore' of teaching. These beliefs and misconceptions have been responsible for the misdirection of vast quantities of resources, time and attention – often with either minimal or even negative impact. In this chapter, Dr Kerry Hempenstall posits that the best bulwark against such destructive myths is evidence-informed practice. He evaluates a wide range of approaches to teaching literacy against the criterion of peer-reviewed evidence, and draws objective conclusions about how we should be investing our resources. Be prepared to be challenged and most importantly, to think about what evidence teachers need in order to evaluate whether a particular teaching approach is effective.

Author bio-sketch:

Dr. Kerry Hempenstall is a teacher and educational psychologist formerly in the Division of Psychology, RMIT University, where he had been an Associate Professor and Manager of the Educational Psychology division of the RMIT Psychology Clinic. In addition to undergraduate and postgraduate lecturing, he provided clinical training for masters and doctoral students in the assessment and remediation of children's and adults' educational problems.

He is now in an honorary position as Senior Industry Fellow, School of Education, RMIT University. Prior to his commencement with RMIT in 1992, he had spent more than 20 years with the Victorian Education Department as a secondary teacher, and educational psychologist.

Kerry has been active in presenting workshops and papers at conferences, and he continues to publish in education journals (e.g. the Australian of Learning Difficulties). He also participates in educational online forums, such as the DDOL network for academics interested in literacy and effective teaching. He has also published numerous papers on educational topics: www.bit.ly/36TkjH6

If not evidence... what then?

Education has long been subjected to teaching programs adopted through unreliable means: through intuition, personal testimonials, hype, ideology, published anecdotes, sales brochures, neuroglitter, etc.[1] An assumption throughout this chapter is that the education of our children would be dramatically enhanced were evidence-based practices to become the norm. A number education programs are viewed through the prism of empirical research.

What is evidence-based practice?

Evidence-based practice involves conscientious, explicit, and judicious use of the best available evidence in making decisions (Sackett, 2000). Individuals, both laypeople and professionals, typically use some form of evidence in making decisions – if only their past experience. EBP raises the issue of what that evidence is and, in particular, how strong it might be (Barends et al., 2014; Sackett, 2000). Evidence-based practitioners seek to improve the quality of the evidence used and condition their decisions and practices on the confidence that the evidence warrants. Importantly, effective EBP practice requires a commitment to continuous practice improvement and lifelong learning (Straus et al., 2005, p. 5).[2]

There have been strong moves around the world towards evidence-based practice in numerous fields in recent years. A simple Google search on 'evidence-based practice' produced 73,000,000 hits in 2006[3] and 502,000,000 hits in 2019. A recent search on 'evidence-based practice in education' produced 384,000,000 hits.

Acknowledgement of the importance of EBP has risen, however, this has not necessarily led to wholesale changes in the beliefs and practices of policy makers, teacher education faculties, or teachers in classrooms. Most teachers-in-training are not exposed to either the principles of EBP or to the practices that have been shown to be beneficial to student learning.[4, 5]

The adoption of evidence-based practice (EBP) in industry and some other professions is far advanced in comparison to its use in education. The resistance displayed by some in education towards the adoption of EBP has also been evident in the early stages of its eventual acceptance by other professions, such as medicine and psychology.[1] However, as these principles have been promoted in those two fields since the early '90s, a new generation of practitioners have been exposed to EBP as the normal standard for practice. This has occurred among young practitioners because their pre-service training has emphasised the centrality of evidence in competent practice.

There are a number of reasons why this change has been slow in education, among them a science-averse culture endemic among education policy makers and teacher education faculties.[1, 4, 5]

A consequence is the likelihood of educators developing beliefs that are unsupported by evidence, and are detrimental to effective instruction, in particular for struggling students. For example, a survey of teachers in Great Britain and the Netherlands in 2012[6] found that at least 80% of the teachers agreed with statements supportive of incorporating in their teaching learning styles, hemispheric dominance, and coordination exercises to aid the integration of the left and right hemispheres. Among teacher educators, similar issues arise. In one study,[7] more than 80% believed that the most appropriate role of a teacher is to be a learning facilitator, while only 11% saw a role for explicit teaching.

How might we avoid such errors of judgment?

There are two major areas of interest in judging whether an approach has merit. The first is to consider whether the theoretical constructs behind the approach are consistent with the research consensus about a given educational issue. This is not a perfect pass-fail criterion, as occasionally a new paradigm makes earlier theories redundant. However, that is rare in education. In the case of some of the approaches – say visual or auditory perceptual issues – one would acknowledge that they at least sound plausible (to a greater or lesser degree) and are known to have an association with reading.

The second criterion goes beyond theoretical relevance, and concerns whether addressing a reading problem by intervening with a program has a beneficial impact. The assumption in this chapter is that using these two criteria offers a bulwark against the adoption of ineffective approaches to literacy.

At the empirical level, Stanovich and Stanovich[8] proposed that competing claims to knowledge should be evaluated according to three criteria. First, findings should be published in refereed journals. Second, the findings have been replicated by independent researchers. Third, there is a consensus within the appropriate research community about the reliability and validity of the various findings. Together these constitute converging evidence criteria. Although the use of these criteria does not produce infallibility, it does offer strong consumer protection against spurious claims to knowledge.

So what are these practices that have insufficient research to justify their inclusion as literacy programs? They include the three-cueing approach, learning styles, sensory processing programs, working memory training such as Cogmed, literacy through music, and 'brain training' approaches such as Arrowmith, BrainGym and Dore.

The three-cueing system

One might expect that after the publication of numerous authoritative reports on skilled reading and how to promote it (such as that of the National Reading Panel, 2000[9]) this tired hypothesis would have been long ago assigned to the history folder. However, a cursory search for the three-cueing term produces many examples of it being endorsed by school districts, education departments, teacher training institutions and school documents.[10] It is arguably the most egregious of all the myths in education because it has been imposed upon – and provided misdirection to – many millions of students for decades.

The three-cueing system and its associated assessment system, miscue analysis and running records are predicated upon the notion that skilled reading is dependent upon the coordinated use of three information sources: semantic, syntactic and graphophonic cues. The three cues are in decreasing order of importance, and their use among skilled readers is considered to be automatic.[11]

This conception of reading development is erroneous[11] and the activities of teachers employing its recommendations inadvertently subvert the reading progress of students, and in particular, of those students who do not readily progress without appropriate assistance.[12, 13, 14, 15]

It is struggling readers who attempt to use context, largely because they lack the decoding skills and orthographic knowledge of good readers.[16] Contextual guessing is a highly inaccurate process; even strong readers guess correctly only one word in four through contextual cues.[17] However, they soon learn that attention to word structure more quickly and reliably supplies the word's pronunciation.[18] Eye movement studies show that fluent readers recognise most words in a few tenths of a second,[19, 20] far faster than complex syntactic and semantic analyses can be performed. The error made by whole language theorists was to confuse the desired outcome of reading instruction – a capacity to grasp the meaning of a text – with the process of achieving that end. In order to comprehend meaning, the student must first learn to understand the code.[21]

Thus the presumption that skilled readers employ contextual cues as the major strategy in *decoding* is not supported by evidence. There is, however, no dispute about the value of contextual cues in assisting readers to gain *meaning* from text.[19] The comprehension of a phrase, clause, sentence, or passage is dependent on attention to its construction (syntax) and also to the meaning of the text surrounding it (semantics). The critical issue here is the erroneous assertion that the use of contextual strategies is beneficial in the *identification* of words, and that skilled readers make use of these strategies routinely.

Learning styles

Learning styles originated with the child study movement of the early 1900s.[22] There have been about 30 different models; however, the most popular is that individuals vary in their optimal learning styles emphasising either visual, auditory, or kinaesthetic senses.[23] Moreover, it is asserted that these styles can be validly and reliably measured, and that teaching to an individual's learning style leads to improved academic outcomes.[24]

More than 30 years ago, Knight[25] summarised existing research demonstrating how modality usage is actually unstable, varying with task demands rather than being relatively fixed as one would expect a style to be. Additionally, none of the 13 most common learning style measures meets acceptable psychometric standards: internal consistency, test-retest reliability, construct validity and predictive validity.[23, 26, 27]

So, if tests are unable to reliably identify a learning style then perhaps teachers can recognise their student's style, or perhaps students themselves can be relied upon to accurately identify a style. A recent study noted that student-nominated preference did not align with the VAK assessed style.[28] Additionally, teachers and their students are often not in agreement about the students' own styles.[29] More recent experimental research has also found no effect of learning styles on academic attainment.[30-37] Of the research published in support of learning styles, most have been correlational studies that could not demonstrate causation.[38]

In 2017, more than 30 neuroscientists and educationalists produced a letter to The Guardian,[39] noting that empirical studies of the effectiveness of learning styles have consistently found little or no evidence to support the decision to match teaching material to an individual's purported learning style. Furthermore, it is clear that the nature of the task best determines the optimal mode(s) of instruction.[40, 41]

While there is considerable research to show that many teachers believe in the notion of learning styles, it is not so clear what proportion of teachers actually put this belief into action in their classrooms.

Process training

The history of education is littered with claims of resolving educational problems by improving underlying processes presumed to be important, for example: visual perception, balance, primitive reflexes, auditory processing speed, perceptual motor skill, brain patterns, working memory and so on. Generally speaking, these endeavours have not been rewarded.[42] In some cases, the interventions didn't improve the underlying processes, in some they did improve the underlying processes but had no impact on reading skill. In others, there were difficulties in accurately assessing the processes and/or teaching them effectively. Many have followed this trail – remove the apparent obstacle to learning and attainment will then readily occur. However, this underlying process approach has so far represented an educational cul-de-sac.

> Process training has always made the phoenix look like a bedraggled sparrow. You cannot kill it. It simply bides its time in exile after being dislodged by one of history's periodic attacks upon it and then returns, wearing disguises or carrying new noms de plume, as it were, but consisting of the same old ideas, doing business much in the same old ways.[43]

The perceptual-motor deficit theory of dyslexia was very strong in the 1960s and 1970s, and an industry of intervention programs erupted. Though some children became adept at skills such as drawing lines accurately within parallel boundaries, there was no reliable impact on reading progress.[1] In fact the meta-analysis performed by Kavale and Forness[28] produced an overall effect size for perceptual-motor training of 0.08, which is a very small effect.[44] What was not readily apparent at that time was that learning to read was the most effective way to master many of those skills, hence valuable instructional time was better spent on the target task. 'If the goal is for children to learn a particular skill (like reading), it is more efficient to teach it directly than to expect it to transfer from other learning' (p. 107).[45] Kavale's summary of research into direct instruction[46] concluded that direct instruction in reading is five to ten times more effective for struggling students than are practices aimed at altering mostly unobservable processes such as perception.

More recently there was a review of the evidence generally for such cognitively focused aptitude-treatment interactions for low progress students.

The conclusions?

> There was no evidence for the notion that when a treatment is matched to a cognitive deficit it produces better effects [...]. Scientific evidence does not justify practitioners' use of cognitively focused instruction to accelerate the academic progress of low-performing children with or without apparent cognitive deficits and an SLD label. At the same time, research does not support 'shutting the door' on the possibility that cognitively focused interventions may eventually prove useful to chronically non-responsive students in rigorous efficacy trials (p.101-102).[47]

As the above authors note, the history of failure of underlying processing approaches doesn't mean that the next big thing can't work. It simply means that an array of strong empirical, independent evidence is necessary, because to back yet another lame horse has serious implications for struggling students. Even if the interventions are non-harmful, there is an opportunity-cost for students (and often a financial cost to parents), and a residue of negative emotion for both parents and child when the approach has no discernible effect.

Do memory-training programs improve the learning of academic skills?

Many students have difficulty in maintaining information in working memory (WM) for long enough and with sufficient clarity to make productive use of it. They may also struggle to sustain sufficient attention on tasks to enable their prompt completion. It is acknowledged that phonological recoding in working memory is a significant contributor to reading progress.[48] Thus, one could envisage that directly improving working memory may offer a shortcut to increased attainment in academic tasks such as reading.[49]

There are numerous (usually) computer-based WM training programs (such as Cogmed) intended to stimulate general cognitive change by addressing working memory and attention. The programs involve a variety of tasks designed to be enjoyable while training and testing individuals' working memory. It is usual to incorporate incremental increases in item difficulty, adjusted according to the students' performance. Computer-based training offers an attractive, accessible vehicle for those who are deemed in need.

It is recognised that there is an established relationship between WM and academic skills, in which adequate WM is considered a pre-condition. Thus, the possibility that directly training under-developed WM might also influence higher cognition is worthy of investigation.[50] It was been noted earlier, however, that previous attempts to train a range of underlying processes in order to boost academic skills has not been as productive as directly and explicitly teaching the requisite skills. The WM training approach is predicated upon the brain's neuroplasticity, such that the stimulation caused by the repeated practice on relevant tasks produces beneficial functional and anatomical changes in the brain's neural structure and function.[51] It has been proposed that these changes will produce improvements in a variety of characteristics, such as WM, intelligence, concentration, endurance, impulse control and emotional regulation.[52] It is also expected that these changes will be evident not only on the trained tasks, but also on other tasks and in other settings, such as those required in academic and professional domains. It is critical that any training benefits will transfer to other tasks measuring non-trained cognitive functions important in everyday life functioning, such as literacy.[53]

The working memory training programs have been shown to improve working memory on trained tasks, and to a lesser extent on tasks similar to those taught, but the benefits have not been demonstrated to generalise to academic learning or to be maintained over long periods.[54]

Even positive results have been inconsistent within and across studies. Unfortunately, the few studies with positive findings have been criticised on a number of methodological grounds, including measurement instrument difficulties, a lack of control groups (especially active controls), small sample sizes and insufficient studies employing random assignment.[55, 56] There is also a concern that the proposed mechanism for producing improvement has not been clearly demonstrated to be the cause of any assessed improvement. Alternative explanations could include placebo effect through motivational change because of the increased interest and attention to the participant's performance.[57] Recent reviews and meta-analyses conclude that working memory training has yet to be shown to benefit the learning of academic skills such as reading.[58-66]

There is some continuing research focused upon specific groups, such as those with ADHD, learning disabilities, cochlear implants, those born preterm, and those with a brain injury or dementia.[67-72] More definitive conclusions may be reachable in the next few years as study quality and quantity improves.

> Working-memory training as currently implemented does not work. One hundred years of research on basic memory phenomena has discovered many procedures that do! (p. 190)[73]

Cogmed Working Memory Training is one commercial example. There is not enough supportive research on this intervention that meets the scientific standards that could justify claims of effectiveness.[74] The findings of other research[75, 76] and a recent meta-analysis of 50 studies were consistent with the results of earlier research that near-zero effects are found in far-transfer measures of academic achievement, despite small to medium effects in memory tasks similar to those practised.[77]

Rapid auditory temporal processing (RATP) and Fast ForWord

This sounds plausible as a possible cause of reading problems as auditory frequency discrimination skills are correlated with reading. Sensitivity to various dimensions of an auditory signal, specifically to frequency discrimination (FD), has been shown to be related to higher linguistic abilities. For example, reading skills are associated with discrimination thresholds, in the general population and in individuals with specific language impairment and/or dyslexia. Furthermore, low FD at infancy predict subsequent linguistic difficulties.[78]

Fast ForWord Language[79] is designed to help children's reading and spoken language by training their memory, attention, processing and sequencing. Children train for three to five days per week, for 8 to 12 weeks. The modified speech in the Fast ForWord exercises is designed to ameliorate the rapid auditory processing deficit. The subsequently enhanced frequency discrimination is expected to improve the phonological processing of language (a key skill for reading), while also having a positive impact on other cognitive and reading skills. There is evidence that the training does benefit pitch discrimination tasks similar to the trained protocol.

Study quality has presented difficulties, such that lower quality studies have tended to find significant effects on reading.[80] After screening 130 evaluation studies for quality, and a meta-analysis[81] of the six well-designed interventions, the authors concluded that there was no evidence for the effectiveness of Fast ForWord as a treatment for children's reading or expressive or receptive vocabulary weaknesses. Similarly, Sisson's systematic review of 31 studies found no significant effects on academic performance.[82]

When two variables A and B are found to be correlated, presuming that A causes B is often a faulty assumption. RATP appears to be an example of a process that is related to both phonology and dyslexia, and RATP can be enhanced, but improving it doesn't appear to have any impact on reading. Any learning that has occurred is limited to the auditory processing, and doesn't transfer to reading.[78, 83]

So, it may be that training specifically with acoustically modified speech is not necessary to remediate language impairments. Doing so appears to be an unnecessary addition to simply providing validated literacy interventions.[84]

Vision problems

Two of the main interventions for dyslexia that emphasise the treatment of visual deficits are behavioural optometry and Irlen lenses. Each claims that the visual focus of their interventions also has a direct impact upon reading development.

Behavioural optometry

The 19th century origins of behavioural optometry involved eye exercises for the treatment of strabismus (crossed eyes). In more recent times, it has expanded the range of eye conditions for which it offers intervention, employing prisms, lenses, convergence exercises, and computerised training programs. The broadening of its scope to include treatment for educational problems, such as dyslexia, has created great controversy because of the paucity of evidence underpinning the claims.

The criticisms of the behavioural optometry claims about dyslexia are extensive. However, major concerns include: the absence of well-designed studies;[85] the failure of studies to produce evidence of visual processing being causal to reading difficulties[86] (indeed, there has been evidence that they may be consequential to reading difficulties);[87, 88] the variation across studies in the definition of dyslexia employed, and hence the techniques used to assess dyslexia and reading;[89] the absence of reliable effects on reading of behavioural optometry interventions;[90,91] some of the tests used to test accommodation, convergence and eye tracking are lacking in validity and reliability;[92] learning to read is either unrelated to magnocellular disturbance[93, 94, 95] or learning to read is followed by changes in the magnocellular system, and not vice versa;[96] not all students with dyslexia have these deficits,[97] and some typically developing readers also have visual deficits.[98,99] For example, in the Creavin et al. study of 5822 students, 80% of the dyslexia cohort displayed normal ophthalmic results in each of the tests involved; relevant major national bodies actively discourage the use of behavioural optometry for educational interventions;[90, 100, 101] in studies reporting that short-term prism correction aided reading, a placebo explanation is likely as the effect appears to be ephemeral.[102] In contrast to the lack of evidence for visual intervention, instruction in phonics, word analysis, reading fluency and comprehension for dyslexia has an acknowledged positive impact.[103, 104, 105]

Criticism of the lack of evidence for a role for behavioural optometry in reading difficulty does not extend to those students who display refractive errors, such as myopia (nearsightedness) and hyperopia (farsightedness), as it is accepted that uncorrected visual acuity weakness may compromise reading proficiency, and simple correction with eyeglasses is all that is required to eliminate that obstacle, and assist subsequent reading development.[106] The consensus among non-aligned researchers is that vision-based treatment for academic problems, and in particular, dyslexia, does not have the evidence-base to support its use. In this period, in education in which evidence-based practice is strongly endorsed, it would not be in students' best interests to recommend such interventions for them.

Scotopic sensitivity and Irlen lens

Helen Irlen was a psychologist working with adults with reading difficulties during the 1980s. She believed that she had detected a visual stress problem in many of these adults that involved undue sensitivity to particular light frequencies. The frequencies varied among the individuals, and she developed assessment intended to determine which frequencies were problematic for each client. She named the visual condition Scotopic Sensitivity Syndrome (also referred to as Irlen Syndrome), and began to prescribe coloured lenses or overlays to reduce this visual stress.

Irlen asserted that a precise colour (frequency) is needed to treat Irlen Syndrome. One would anticipate that the choice of colour would be similar if a person was re-assessed. However, a recent study[107] observed that only one third of candidates chose the same colour overlay on re-assessment at 25 days. More males preferred blue and green lenses, whereas females mainly preferred pink and purple. Griffiths et al. reported that 63% had ceased wearing their lenses after three weeks.[108] The internal validity and reliability of the Irlen assessment scales have not been published in any refereed journal.

The approach remains controversial in the research community, both because it has been argued that no such Scotopic Sensitivity Syndrome (SSS) exists[109] and that the treatment has not been demonstrated to be effective in well-designed studies.[107, 108, 110, 111] Further compromising the educational relevance of SSS, is that scotopic sensitivity has also been reported among typically developing readers.[112]

As with behavioural optometry, the use of Irlen lenses and overlays is discouraged by seven relevant official bodies[100] because of the absence of theoretical salience, contentious assessment tools, poor research designs and an absence of clear empirically supported student reading outcomes. However, Irlen lenses remain accepted as a viable treatment for dyslexia by many teachers.[113, 114]

Arrowsmith

Arrowsmith offers a several year full-time learning program employing neuroscience to reach the supposed underlying causes of learning disabilities. It provides exercises designed to reach and enhance the functioning of 19 specific brain areas they consider to be critical in learning. It is an intense, for-profit program that makes strong claims for its effectiveness:

[U]pon completion, and with the attendant improved cognitive capacities, students are able to participate in a full academic curriculum at their appropriate grade level without the need for resource support or curriculum modification.[115]

However, there is simply no evidence published in refereed journals, despite the program having been developed more than 30 years ago:

At the moment, the effect of the Arrowsmith program on skills such as reading and writing has not been tested in a randomised control trial, and so there is no direct evidence for their claims.[116]

The intensity and several years duration of a program that does not teach academic skills and knowledge also raises the question as to how students would manage on their return to a regular education program having missed so much conventional education.[117]

In 2019, Arrowsmith produced a 'Summary of Research Studies on the Arrowsmith Program as Presented by Researchers from UBC and SIU'.[118] Data was collected and analysed from students in the Arrowsmith Program in six schools. There are no detailed results available, though they were classed as significant positive changes in a number of cognitive domains. There is no indication as yet of any journal submission or publication.

Brain Gym

Brain Gym was created in the 1970s to assist learning disabled children and adults. The authors championed the use of 26 specific exercises to repattern the brain, and called the process educational kinesiology. It claims 'a sound basis in neuroscience',[119] and consists of 'integrated, cross-lateral, balance-requiring movements that mechanically activate both hemispheres of the brain via the motor and sensory cortexes, stimulate the vestibular (balance) system for equilibrium, and decrease the fight or flight mechanism'.[119]

Theoretically, Brain Gym derives from the long discredited notions of mixed cerebral dominance, perceptual motor training and neurological repatterning.[120] Most of the published studies are in a dedicated Brain Gym journal. A review of both the theoretical foundations of Brain Gym and the associated peer-reviewed research studies failed to support the contentions of the promoters of Brain Gym. Hyatt concluded:[121]

[…] articles contained serious methodological flaws. […] data did not demonstrate that the Brain Gym® activities were superior to no treatment at all. […] clearly failed to support claims that Brain Gym® movements were effective interventions for academic learning.

Subsequent reviews have expressed similar concerns about the program, and the strong impact of its marketing strategies.[122] They have led to a too ready acceptance by both schools and parents without demonstrating that this faith is deserved.[123]

DORE

The Dore (aka DDAT) program is based upon the belief that a delay in cerebellum development is responsible for such varied conditions as attention-deficit hyperactivity disorder, dyslexia, dyspraxia, and Asperger's syndrome. Additionally, it claims that a series of prescribed exercises can enhance cerebellar growth, thereby ameliorating these difficulties.[124] Exercises included catching beanbags while standing on a cushion on one leg. The program was controversial from its commencement in the early years of this century, and excited much media attention at the time. The authors' evaluative research was dismissed as being flawed in design. For example, the original 2003 study[125] did not contain an active control group, and the groups were not matched.[126, 127]

There has not been any independent evidence published for the claimed gains in literacy for the specified populations,[128] and the Dore theory and practice has been heavily criticised.[123, 129, 130, 131]

In 2009, the Advertising Standards Authority[132] in the UK ordered Wynford Dore to remove the claims used in his advertising. The program has been less prominent in recent years, though it continues to market its program to parents. There also remains a Dore website that advertises services in the USA.[133] Interestingly, the button to click for a list of the Independent Peer-Reviewed Published research is non-functioning. The site also claims that: 'New participants are currently being enrolled in the United States, the United Kingdom, South Africa, Taiwan, New Zealand and China.'[133] It is not clear whether the site is actually current.

One Dore closes... Recently noted on the blog of Dorothy Bishop[132] was reference to a newer program with some similarities to Dore currently being marketed in the UK to schools (rather than to parents). It is called STEP Physical Literacy, and Bishop noted:

> [...] the underlying theory is similar, namely that cerebellar training will improve skills beyond motor skills. The idea that training motor skills will produce effects that generalise to other aspects of development is dubious because the cerebellum is a complex organ subserving a range of functions and controlled studies typically find that training effects are task-specific.

The Dore program is another example of a purported solution to important problems that fails at both the theoretical and empirical level of evidence.

Music training

Many people – including children – find listening to music pleasurable. However, it is the possible side benefits of music tuition that have created significant research and media interest. If it could be shown that learning music transfers to reading development, then music education would become a more attractive curriculum option in school settings, and an additional focus for parents determined to take every opportunity to enhance their children's development.

Numerous studies have found a correlation between music training and reading skill, but it needs to be shown that music training can actually transfer to reading improvement. The explanation for the association may be simply that brighter individuals are more likely to engage in music programs, and there is evidence that this is so.[134]

Some studies fail to employ active control groups and consequently cannot rule out such potential confounds.[135, 136] Larger effects have tended to be reported in lower quality studies.[137] High quality research reports little or no evidence for a transfer effect.[136, 137, 138, 139] To date, there have been too few randomised control trials (RCTs) to clarify if, and under what conditions, music training might produce reading skill enhancement.[136, 140, 141]

For students whose reading is at risk, powerful effects are already known to occur from the explicit, systematic teaching of the critical components of the reading process. Music training programs have numerous cultural benefits for participants. However, if the purpose for their introduction is to have a direct and significant impact on academic outcomes, such as reading, music training is not recommended based upon current evidence.

Conclusion

So, what are we to make of the presence and success of many of these ineffective programs?

> We believe it is imperative for educators to 'critically read and analyze the research in order to separate the wheat from the chaff' (Wolfe & Brandt, 1998, p. 10). The problem, however, is that parents and educators alike often lack discriminative ability – 'the ability to know and understand what works effectively, what does not work effectively, and the ability to tell the difference' (Mostert, 1999-2000, p. 119). Along with the challenge

to become critical consumers, teacher preparation programs should re-examine how they equip pre-service teachers to critically examine special education literature, and, similarly, parents and communities need much more accurate information to avoid promises for money that are completely unsustainable.[142]

That being said, it is important to remember the aphorism 'absence of evidence is not evidence of absence'. It is conceivable that some of these programs may achieve acceptance when sufficient high-quality research is available. One way to address the question of what currently works is to stay in touch with journals germane to one's education domain. A less onerous option is to maintain contact with resources that outline evidence-based practice. It has also been suggested that including academic instruction on neuroscience during undergraduate education courses would assist in inoculating prospective teachers from being drawn to neuromyths.[143]

References

1. Carnine, D. (2000) *Why education experts resist effective practices (and what it would take to make education more like medicine)*. Washington, DC: Fordham Foundation. Retrieved from: www.edexcellence.net/library/carnine.html

2. Rousseau, D. M. and Gunia, B. C. (2015) 'Evidence-based practice: The psychology of EBP implementation', *Annual Review of Psychology* 67 pp. 667-692.

3. Hempenstall, K. (2006) What does evidence-based practice in education mean? *Australian Journal of Learning Disabilities* 11 (2) pp. 83-92.

4. Wijekumar, K., Beerwinkle, A. L., Harris, K. R. and Graham, S. (2019) 'Etiology of teacher knowledge and instructional skills for literacy at the upper elementary grades', *Annals of Dyslexia* 69 (1) pp. 5-20.

5. Stephenson, J. (2018) 'A systematic review of the research on the knowledge and skills of Australian preservice teachers', *Australian Journal of Teacher Education* 43 (4) pp. 121-137.

6. Dekker, S., Lee, N. C., Howard-Jones, P. and Jolles, J. (2012) 'Neuromyths in education: prevalence and predictors of misconceptions among teachers', *Frontiers of Psychology* 3 p. 429.

7. Farkas, S. and Duffett, A. (2011) 'Cracks in the ivory tower? The views of education professors circa 2010', *Thomas B. Fordham Institute* [Online], 21 October. Retrieved from www.bit.ly/2mVRFmE

8. Stanovich, P. J. and Stanovich, K. E. (2003) *Using Research and Reason in Education: How Teachers Can Use Scientifically Based Research to Make Curricular & Instructional Decisions*. Jessup, MD: The National Institute for Literacy. Retrieved from: www.bit.ly/2oq2rBR

9. National Reading Panel (2000) *Teaching children to read: An evidence-based assessment of the scientific research literature on reading and its implications for reading instruction*. Washington, DC: U.S. Department of Health and Human Services.

10. Seidenberg, M. (2017). *Language at the speed of sight: How we read, why so many can't, and what can be done about it* (first edition). New York, NY: Basic Books.

11. Hempenstall, K. (2003) 'The three-cueing system: Trojan horse?', *Australian Journal of Learning Disabilities* 8 (2) pp. 15-23.

12. Beatty, L. and Care, E. (2009) 'Learning from their miscues: Differences across reading ability and text difficulty', *Journal of Language and Literacy* 32 (3) pp. 226-244.

13. Clifton, C. E., Ferreira, F., Henderson, J. M., Inhoff, A. W., Liversedge, S., Reichle, E. D. and Schotter, E. R. (2016). 'Eye movements in reading and information processing: Keith Rayner's 40 year legacy', *Journal of Memory and Language* 86 pp. 1-19.

14. Wren, S. (2008) *Reading and the three cueing systems. Topics in Early Reading Coherence, 141.5.* Washington, DC: Southwest Educational Development Laboratory.

15. Chapman, J. W., Arrow, A. W., Braid, C., Greaney, K. T. and Tunmer, W. E. (2018) *Enhancing literacy learning outcomes for beginning readers: Research results and teaching strategies.* Palmerston North, New Zealand: College of Humanities and Social Sciences Massey University. Retrieved from: www.bit.ly/2nz2awA

16. Nicholson, T. (1991) 'Do children read words better in context or in lists? A classic study revisited', *Journal of Educational Psychology* 82 pp. 444-450.

17. Gough, P. B. (1993) 'The beginning of decoding', *Reading and Writing: An Interdisciplinary Journal* 5 pp. 181-192.

18. Perfetti, C. A. (1985) *Reading ability.* New York, NY: Oxford.

19. Stanovich, K. E. (1980) 'Toward an interactive-compensatory model of individual differences in the development of reading fluency', *Reading Research Quarterly* 26 pp. 32-71.

20. Ibid (n 3)

21. Foorman, B. R. (1995) 'Research on "the Great Debate" – Code-oriented versus Whole Language approaches to reading instruction', *School Psychology Review* 24 pp. 376-392.

22. Stone, J. E. and Clements, A. (1998) 'Research and innovation: Let the buyer beware', in Spillane, R. R. and Regnier, P. (eds) *The superintendent of the future.* Gaithersburg, MD: Aspen Publishers, pp. 59-97.

23. Coffield, F., Moseley, D., Hall, E. and Ecclestone, K. (2004) *Learning styles and pedagogy in post-16 learning: A systematic and critical review.* London: Learning and Skills Research Centre.

24. Cuevas, J. and Dawson, B. L. (2018) 'A test of two alternative cognitive processing models: Learning styles and dual coding', *Theory and Research in Education* 16 (1) pp. 40–64.

25. Knight, D. (1997) 'Learning styles and accelerative learning: An appraisal', *Australian Journal of Learning Disabilities* 2 pp. 25-28.

26. Snider, V. E. (1992) 'Learning styles and learning to read: A critique', *Remedial and Special Education* 13 (1) pp. 6-18.

27. Graham, N. A. and Kershner, J. R. (1996) 'Reading styles in children with dyslexia – a neuropsychological evaluation of modality preference on the Reading Style Inventory', *Learning Disability Quarterly* 19 pp. 233-240.

28. Husmann, P. R. and O'Loughlin, V. D. (2019) 'Another nail in the coffin for learning styles? Disparities among undergraduate anatomy students' study strategies, class performance, and reported VARK learning styles', *Anatomical Sciences Education* 12 pp. 6-19.

29. Papadatou-Pastou, M., Gritzali, M. and Barrable, A. (2018) 'The learning styles educational neuromyth: Lack of agreement between teachers' judgments, self-assessment, and students' intelligence', *Frontiers in Education* [Online], 29 November. Retrieved from: www.bit.ly/2nxcy81

30. Allcock, S. J. and Hulme, J. A. (2010) 'Learning styles in the classroom: Educational benefit or planning exercise?', *Psychology Teaching Review* 16 (2) pp. 67-79.

31. Choi, I., Lee, S. J. and Kang, J. (2009) 'Implementing a case-based e-learning environment in a lecture oriented anesthesiology class: Do learning styles matter in complex problem solving over time?', *British Journal of Educational Technology* 40 (5) pp. 933-947.

32. Kappe, F. R., Boekholt, L., den Rooyen, C. and Van der Filer, H. (2009) 'A predictive validity study of the Learning Style Questionnaire (LSQ) using multiple, specific learning criteria', *Learning and Individual Differences* 19 (4) pp. 464-467.

33. Kirschner, P. A. (2017) 'Stop propagating the learning styles myth', *Computers & Education* 106 pp. 166-171.

34. Kozub, R. M. (2010) 'An ANOVA analysis of the relationships between business students' learning styles and effectiveness of web based instruction', *American Journal of Business Education* 3 (3) pp. 89-98.

35. Rogowsky, B. A., Calhoun, B. M. and Tallal, P. (2015) 'Matching learning style to instructional method: Effects on comprehension', *Journal of Educational Psychology* 107 (1) pp. 64-78.

36. Sankey, M. D., Birch, D. and Gardiner, M. W. (2011) 'The impact of multiple representations of content using multimedia on learning outcomes across learning styles and modal preferences', *International Journal of Education & Development using Information & Communication Technology* 7 (3) pp. 18-35.

37. Zachari, N. Z. (2011) 'The effect of learning style on preference for web-based courses and learning outcomes', *British Journal of Educational Technology* 42 (5) pp. 790-800.

38. Cuevas, J. and Dawson, B. L. (2018) 'A test of two alternative cognitive processing models: Learning styles and dual coding', *Theory and Research in Education* 16 (1) pp. 40-64. Retrieved from: www.bit.ly/2pgw09t

39. Hood, B. et al. (2017) 'No evidence to back idea of learning styles', *The Guardian* [Online], 12 March. Retrieved from: www.bit.ly/2nvR1qi

40. Kavale, K. A. and Forness, S. R. (1987) 'Substance over style: Assessing the efficacy of modality testing and teaching', *Exceptional Children* 54 pp. 228-239.

41. Pashler, H., McDaniel, M., Rohrer, D. and Bjork, R. (2009) 'Learning styles: Concepts and evidence', *Psychological Science in the Public Interest* 9 pp. 105-119.

42. Arter, J. A. and Jenkins, J. R. (1979) 'Differential diagnosis—Prescriptive teaching: A critical appraisal', *Review of Educational Research* 49 pp. 517-555.

43. Mann, L. (1979) On the trail of process. New York, NY: Grune & Stratton, p. 539.

44. Cohen, J. (1988) *Statistical power analysis for the behavioural sciences* (second edition). Hillsdale, NJ: Lawrence Erlbaum.

45. Singer, H. and Balow, I. H. (1981) 'Overcoming educational disadvantageness', in Guthrie, J. T. (ed), *Comprehension and teaching: Research review*. Newark, DE: International Reading Association.

46. Kavale, K. A. (1990) 'Variances & verities in learning disability interventions', in Scruggs, T. and Wong, B. (eds) *Intervention research in learning disabilities*. New York, NY: Springer Verlag, pp. 3-33.

47. Fuchs, D., Hale, J. B. and Kearns, D. M. (2011) 'On the importance of a cognitive processing perspective: An introduction', *Journal of Learning Disabilities* 44 (2) pp. 99-104.

48. Kim, Y. S. G. and Petscher, Y. (2016) 'Prosodic sensitivity and reading: An investigation of pathways of relations using a latent variable approach', *Journal of Educational Psychology* 108 (5) pp. 630-645.

49. Lervag, A., Hulme, C. and Melby-Lervag, M. (2017) 'Unpicking the developmental relationship between oral language skills and reading comprehension: It's simple, but complex', *Child Development* 89 (5) pp. 1-18.

50. De Simoni, C. and von Bastian, C. C. (2018) 'Working memory updating and binding training: Bayesian evidence supporting the absence of transfer', *Journal of Experimental Psychology: General* 147 (6) pp. 829-858.

51. Martone, R. (2018) 'Early life experience: It's in your DNA', *Scientific American* [Online], 10 July. Retrieved from: www.bit.ly/2zAG7ea

52. Takeuchi, H., Taki, Y. and Kawashima, R. (2010) 'Effects of working memory training on cognitive functions and neural systems', *Reviews in the Neurosciences* 21 (6) pp. 427-449.

53. Sala, G., Aksayli, N. D., Semir, K., Gondo, Y. and Gobet, F. (2018) 'Working Memory Training Does Not Enhance Older Adults' Cognitive Skills: A Comprehensive Meta-Analysis', *PsyArXiv Reprints* [Online], 23 July. Retrieved from: www.psyarxiv.com/5frzb/

54. Maehler, C., Joerns, C. and Schuchardt, K. (2019) 'Training working memory of children with and without dyslexia', *Children* 6 (3) pp. 1-15.

55. Simons, D. J., Boot, W. R., Charness, N., Gathercole, S. E., Chabris, C. F., Hambrick, D. Z. and Stine-Morrow, E. A. L. (2016) 'Do "brain-training" programs work?', *Psychological Science in the Public Interest* 17 (3) pp. 103-186.

56. Zhao, X., Xu, Y., Fu, J. and Maes, J. H. R (2018). 'Are training and transfer effects of working memory updating training modulated by achievement motivation?' *Memory & Cognition* 46 pp. 398-409.

57. Sala, G., Aksayli, N. D., Tatlidil, K. S., Tatsumi, T., Gondo, Y., and Gobet, F. (2019) 'Near and far transfer in cognitive training: A second-order meta-analysis', *Collabra: Psychology* 5 (1) p. 18.

58. Dougherty, M. R., Hamovitz, T. and Tidwell, J. W. (2016) 'Reevaluating the effectiveness of n-back training on transfer through the Bayesian lens: Support for the null', *Psychonomic Bulletin & Review* 23 pp. 306-316.

59. Jacoby, N. and Ahissar, M. (2015) 'Assessing the applied benefits of perceptual training: Lessons from studies of training working-memory', *Journal of Vision* 15 p. 6.

60. Melby-Lervåg, M. and Hulme, C. (2013) 'Is working memory training effective? A meta-analytic review', *Developmental Psychology* 49 (2) pp. 270-291.

61. Melby-Lervåg, M., Redick, T. S. and Hulme, C. (2016) 'Working memory training does not improve performance on measures of intelligence or other measures of far transfer: Evidence from a meta-analytic review', *Perspectives on Psychological Science* 11 (4) pp. 512-534.

62. Brown, P. C., Roediger, H. L. and McDaniel, M. A. (2014) *Make it stick: The science of successful learning.* Cambridge, MA: Harvard University Press

63. Sala, G. and Gobet, F. (2017) 'Working memory training in typically developing children: A meta-analysis of the available evidence', *Developmental Psychology* 53 (4) pp. 671-685.

64. Schwaighofer, M. Fischer, F. and Bühner, M. (2015) 'Does working memory training transfer? A meta-analysis including training conditions as moderators', *Educational Psychologist* 50 (2) pp. 138-166.

65. Shipstead, Z., Redick, T. S. and Engle, R. W. (2012) 'Is working memory training effective?', *Psychological Bulletin* 138 (4) pp. 628-654.

66. Soveri, A., Antfolk, J., Karlsson, L., Salo, B. and Laine, M. (2017) 'Working memory training revisited: A multi-level meta-analysis of n-back training studies', *Psychonomic Bulletin & Review* 24 pp. 1077-1096.

67. Anderson, P. J., Lee, K. J., Roberts, G., Spencer-Smith, M. M., Thompson, D. K., Seal, M. L., Nosarti, C., Grehan, A., Josev, E. K., Gathercole, S., Doyle, L. W. and Pascoe, L. (2018) 'Long-term academic functioning following Cogmed working memory training for children born extremely preterm: A randomized controlled trial', *Journal of Pediatrics* 202 pp. 92-97.

68. Egeland, J., Aarlien, A. K. and Saunes, B. (2013) 'Few effects of far transfer of working memory training in ADHD: A randomized controlled trial', *PloS One* 8 (10) pp. 1-9.

69. Gray, S. A., Chaban, P., Martinussen, R., Goldberg, R., Gotlieb, H., Kronitz, R., Hockenberry, M. and Tannock, R. (2012) 'Effects of a computerized working memory training program on working memory, attention, and academics in adolescents with severe LD and comorbid ADHD: A randomized controlled trial', *Journal of Child Psychology and Psychiatry* 53 pp. 1277-1284.

70. Karin I. E. and Dahlin, K. I. E. (2010) 'Effects of working memory training on reading in children with special needs', *Reading and Writing* 24 pp. 479-491.

71. Kasper, L. J., Alderson, R. M. and Hudec, K. L. (2012) 'Moderators of working memory deficits in children with attention-deficit/hyperactivity disorder (ADHD): A meta-analytic review', *Clinical Psychology Review* 32 (7) pp. 605-617.

72. Pascoe, L., Roberts, G., Doyle, L. W., Lee, K. J., Thompson, D. K., Seal, M. L., Josev, E. K., Nosarti, C., Gathercole, S. and Anderson, P. J. (2013) 'Preventing academic difficulties in preterm children: A randomised controlled trial of an adaptive working memory training intervention – IMPRINT study', *BMC Pediatrics* 13 pp. 144-156.

73. McCabe, J. A., Redick, T. S. and Engle, R. W. (2016) 'Brain-training pessimism, but applied-memory optimism', *Psychological Science in the Public Interest* 17 (3) pp. 187-191.

74. Shipstead, Z., Hicks, K. L. and Engle, R. W. (2012) 'Cogmed working memory training: Does the evidence support the claims?', *Journal of Applied Research in Memory and Cognition* 1 (3) pp. 185-193.

75. Cortese, S., Ferrin, M., Brandeis, D., Buitelaar, J., Daley, D., Dittmann, R. W., Holtmann, M., Santosh, P., Stevenson, J., Stringaris, A., Zuddas, A. and Sonuga-Barke, E. J. (2015) 'Cognitive training for attention-deficit/hyperactivity disorder: Meta-analysis of clinical and

neuropsychological outcomes from randomized controlled trials', *Journal of American Academy of Child and Adolescent Psychiatry* 54 pp. 164-174.

76. Chacko, A., Bedard, A. C., Marks, D. J., Feirsen, N., Uderman, J. Z., Chimiklis, A., Rajwan, E., Cornwell, M., Anderson, L., Zwilling, A. and Ramon, M. (2013) 'A randomized clinical trial of Cogmed Working Memory Training in school-age children with ADHD: A replication in a diverse sample using a control condition', *Journal of Child Psychology and Psychiatry* 42 (6) pp. 769-783.

77. Aksayli, N. D., Sala, G. and Gobet, F. (2019) 'The cognitive and academic benefits of Cogmed: A meta-analysis', *Educational Research Review* 27 pp. 229-243.

78. Jakoby, H., Raviv, O., Jaffe-Dax, S., Lieder, I. and Ahissar, M. (2019) 'Auditory frequency discrimination is correlated with linguistic skills, but its training does not improve them or other pitch discrimination tasks', *Journal of Experimental Psychology*.

79. What Works Clearinghouse (2013) *Fast ForWord*. Institute of Education Sciences. Retrieved from: www.bit.ly/2paKwPV

80. Dawson, G. and D'Souza, S. (2015) *Behavioural interventions to remediate learning disorders: A technical report*. Auckland, New Zealand: University of Auckland. Retrieved from: www.bit.ly/1J5AQnK

81. Strong, G., Torgerson, C., Torgerson, D., & Hulme, C. (2011) 'A systematic meta-analytic review of evidence for the effectiveness of the 'Fast ForWord' language intervention program', *The Journal of Child Psychology and Psychiatry* 52 (3) pp. 224-235.

82. Sisson, C. B. (2009) *A meta-analytic investigation into the efficacy of Fast ForWord intervention on improving academic performance* (Doctoral dissertation, Regent University, 2009). Dissertation Abstracts International Section A: Humanities and Social Sciences, 69 (12-A) 4633.

83. Tomlin, D. and Vandali, A. (2019) 'Efficacy of a deficit specific auditory training program for remediation of temporal patterning deficits', *International Journal of Audiology* 58 (7) pp. 393-400.

84. Mocan, S. B. and Leacock, T. L. (2009) 'Using Fast ForWord® to support learning to read: A review of the literature', in *E---Learn 2009: Proceedings of the World Conference on E---Learning in Corporate, Government, Healthcare, & Higher Education* pp. 989-997.

85. Barrett, B. T. (2009) 'A critical evaluation of the evidence supporting the practice of behavioural vision therapy', *Ophthalmic Physiological Optics* 29 (1) pp. 4-25.

86. Vellutino, F. R. and Fletcher, J. M. (2005) 'Developmental dyslexia' in Snowling, M. J. and Hulme, C. (eds) *The science of reading: A handbook*. Maldon, MA: Blackwell Publishing, pp. 362-378.

87. Blythe, H., Kirkby, J. and Liversedge, S. (2018) 'Comments on: "What is developmental dyslexia?" Brain Sci. 2018, 8(2), 26-39. The relationship between eye movements and reading difficulties', *Brain Sciences* 8 (6) pp. 100-105.

88. Olulade, O. A., Napoliello, E. M. and Eden, G. F. (2013) 'Abnormal visual motion processing is not a cause of dyslexia', *Neuron* 79 pp. 1-11.

89. Schulte-Körne, G. and Bruder, J. (2010) 'Clinical neurophysiology of visual and auditory processing in dyslexia: A review', *Clinical Neurophysiology* 121 (11) pp. 1794-1809.

90. Mental Health Matters (2009) *Alternative Therapies for ADHD*. Retrieved from: www.bit.ly/2peERs8

91. Rawstron, J. A., Burley, C. D. and Elder, M. J. (2005) 'A systematic review of the applicability and efficacy of eye exercises', *Journal of Pediatrics, Ophthalmology, and Strabismus* 42 (2) pp. 82-88.

92. Larson, S. A. (2018) 'Is oculomotor testing important in developmental dyslexia?', *JAMA Ophthalmology* 136 (10) pp. 1096-1097.

93. American College of Opthalmologists (2009) *POLICY STATEMENT: Learning Disabilities, Dyslexia and Vision.* San Francisco, CA: American Academy of Ophthalmology.

94. Birch, S. and Chase, C. H. (2004) 'Visual and language processing deficits in compensated and impaired dyslexic college students', *Journal of Learning Disabilities* 37 pp. 389 412.

95. Shelley-Tremblay, J. F., Syklawer, S. and Ramkissoon, I. (2011) 'The effects of magno-parvocellular integration training on fluency', *Journal of Behavioral Optometry* 22 (2) pp. 31-37.

96. Georgiou, G. K., Papadopoulos, T. C., Zarouna, E. and Parrila, R. (2012) 'Are auditory and visual processing deficits related to developmental dyslexia?', *Dyslexia* 18 (2) pp. 110-29.

97. Ramus, F., Rosen, S., Dakin, S. C., Day, B. L., Castellote, J. M., White, S. and Frith, U. (2003) 'Theories of developmental dyslexia: Insights from a multiple case study of dyslexic adults', *Brain* 126 pp. 841-865.

98. Creavin, A. L., Lingam, R., Steer, C. and Williams, C. (2015) 'Ophthalmic abnormalities and reading impairment', *Pediatrics* 135 (6) pp. 1057-1065.

99. Quercia, P., Feiss, L. and Michel, C. (2013) 'Developmental dyslexia and vision', *Clinical Ophthalmology* 7 pp. 869-881.

100. Handler, S. M., Fierson, W. M., American Academy of Pediatrics, & the Section on Ophthalmology and Council of Association for Pediatric Ophthalmology and Strabismus, and American Association on Children with Disabilities, American Academy of Ophthalmology, American Certified Orthoptists (2011) 'Joint Technical Report—Learning disabilities, dyslexia, and vision', *Pediatrics* 127 (3) pp. 818-856.

101. Royal Australian and New Zealand College of Ophthalmologists (2017) 'Ophthalmologists condemn Channel 7 report on behavioural optometry', *RANZCO* [website], 10 Auguat. Retrieved from: www.bit.ly/2vosXLf

102. Chung, A. G. and Borsting, E. (2018) 'The impact of short-term prism correction in convergence insufficiency on reading rate and accuracy', *Optometry & Visual Performance* 6 (1) pp. 11-18.

103. Galuschka, K., Ise, E., Krick, K. and Schulte-Korne, G. (2014) 'Effectiveness of treatment approaches for children and adolescents with reading disabilities: A meta-analysis of randomized controlled trials', *PLoS One* 9 (2).

104. Hyatt, K. J., Stephenson, J. and Carter, M. (2009) 'A. review of three controversial educational practices: Perceptual motor programs, sensory integration, and tinted lenses', *Education and Treatment of Children* 3 (2) pp. 313-342.

105. Stein, M. T. (2015) 'Visual training methods are ineffective for dyslexia', *New England Journal of Medicine: Journal Watch* 316 pp. 1238-1243.

106. Slavin, R. E., Collins, M. E., Repka, M. X., Friedman, D. S., Mudie, L. I., Owoeye , J. O. and Madden, N. A. (2018) 'In plain sight: Reading outcomes of providing eyeglasses to disadvantaged children', *Journal of Education for Students Placed at Risk* 23 (3) pp. 250-258.

107. Suttle, C. M., Lawrenson, J. G. and Conway, M. L. (2018) 'Efficacy of coloured overlays and lenses for treating reading difficulty: An overview of systematic reviews', *Clinical and Experimental Optometry* 101 (4) pp. 514-520.

108. Griffiths, P. G., Taylor, R. H, Henderson, L. M. and Barrett, B. T. (2016) 'The effect of coloured overlays and lenses on reading: A systematic review of the literature', *Ophthalmic & Physiological Optics* 36 (5) pp. 519-44.

109. American Optometric Association (2003) *The use of tinted lenses for the treatment of dyslexia and other related reading and learning disorders.* Retrieved from: www.bit.ly/2Iyvpa5

110. Iovino, I., Fletcher, J. M., Breitmeyer, B. G. and Foorman, B. R. (1998) 'Colored overlays for visual perceptual deficits in children with reading disability and attention deficit hyperactivity disorder: Are they differentially effective?', *Journal of Clinical and Experimental Neuropsychology* 20 pp. 791-806.

111. Ritchie, S. J., Sala, S. D. and McIntosh, R. D. (2011) 'Irlen colored overlays do not alleviate reading difficulties', *Pediatrics* 128 (4) pp. 932-938.

112. Lopex, R., Yolton, R. L., Kohl, P., Smith, D. L. and Saxerud, M. H. (1994) 'Comparison of Irlen scotopic sensitivity syndrome test results to academic and visual performance data', *Journal of American Optometric Association* 65 pp. 705-714.

113. Bain, S. K., Brown, K. S. and Jordan, K. R. (2009) 'Teacher candidates' accuracy of beliefs regarding childhood interventions', *The Teacher Educator* 44 (2) pp. 71-89.

114. Washburn, E. K., Mulcahy, C. A., Joshi, M. R. and Binks-Cantrell, E. (2016) 'Teacher knowledge of dyslexia', *Perspectives on Language and Literacy* 42 (4) pp. 9-13.

115. Arrowsmith (2010) *Program Brochure.* Retrieved from: www.bit.ly/2ox0tQ4

116. Castles, A. and McArthur, G. (2012) '"Brain-Training"… or learning, as we like to call it', *The Conversation* [Online], 5 October. Retrieved from: www.bit.ly/2osHYfT

117. Kemp-Koo, D. (2013) *A case study of the Learning Disabilities Association of Saskatchewan (Ldas) Arrowsmith program.* A Thesis submitted to the College of Graduate Studies and Research in Partial Fulfillment of the Requirements for the Degree of Doctor of Philosophy in the Department of Educational Psychology & Special Education University of Saskatchewan Saskatoon.

118. Arrowsmith (2019) *Summary of research studies on the Arrowsmith program.* Retrieved from: www.bit.ly/2nM6w3n

119. Dennison, P. E. (2006) *Brain Gym* and me: Reclaiming the pleasure of learning.* Ventura, CA: Edu-Kinesthetics.

120. Spaulding, L. S., Mostert, M. P. and Beam, A. (2010) 'Is Brain Gym an effective educational intervention?', *Faculty Publications and Presentations*, 148. Retrieved from: www.bit.ly/2nPXxxY

121. Hyatt, J. (2007) 'Brain Gym: Building stronger brains or wishful thinking?', *Remedial and Special Education* 28 (2) pp. 117-124.

122. Kroeze, K., Hyatt, K. J. and Lambert, M. C. (2016) 'Brain Gym: Pseudoscientific practice', *Journal of the American Academy of Special Education Professionals*, pp. 75-80.

123. Sala, S. D. (2009) 'The use and misuse of neuroscience in education', *Cortex* 45 (4) p. 443.

124. Goswami, U. (2004) 'Neuroscience, science and special education', *British Journal of Special Education* 31 (4) pp. 175-183.

125. Reynolds, D. E., Nicolson, R. I. and Hambly, H. (2003) 'Evaluation of an exercise-based treatment for children with reading difficulties', *Dyslexia: An International Journal of Research and Practice* 9 (1) pp. 48-71.

126. Grigg, T. M. (2018) *The influences of a primitive reflex integration programme within the classroom: Teacher/parent perspectives and student results.* A thesis submitted in partial fulfilment of the requirement for the degree of Doctor of Philosophy in Education by School of Health Sciences College of Education, Health and Human Development University of Canterbury, Christchurch, New Zealand. October 2018.

127. Anderson, M. and Reid, C. (2009) 'Don't forget about levels of explanation', *Cortex* 45 (4) pp. 560-561.

128. Hulme, C. and Melby-Lervåg, M. (2015) 'Educational interventions for children's learning difficulties'. in Thapar, A., Pine, D. S., Leckman, J. F., Scott, S., Snowling, M. J. and Taylor, E. (eds) *Rutter's child and adolescent psychiatry* (sixth edition). Hoboken, NJ: Wiley-Blackwell, pp. 533-544.

129. Rack, J. (2003) 'The who, what, why and how of intervention programmes: Comments on the DDAT evaluation', *Dyslexia* 9 (3) pp. 137-139.

130. Bishop, D. V. M. (2007) 'Curing dyslexia and attention-deficit hyperactivity disorder by training motor co-ordination: Miracle or myth?', *Journal of Paediatrics and Child Health* 43 (10) pp. 653-655.

131. Rack, J. P., Snowling, M. J., Hulme, C. and Gibbs, S. (2007) 'No evidence that an exercise-based treatment programme (DDAT) has specific benefits for children with reading difficulties', *Dyslexia* 13 (2) pp. 97-104.

132. Bishop, D. V. M. (2017) 'The STEP Physical Literacy programme: have we been here before?', BishopBlog [Blog], 2 July. Retrieved from: www.bit.ly/2phXNWZ

133. DoreUSA (2012) *Dore USA program.* Retrieved from: www.bit.ly/2mVucSx

134. Sala, G. and Gobet, F. (2018) 'Elvis has left the building: Correlational but not causal relationship between music skill and cognitive ability', *Proceedings of the 41st Annual Meeting of the Cognitive Science Society, Montreal, Canada.*

135. Mehr, S. A., Schachner, A., Katz, R. C. and Spelke, E. S. (2013) Two randomized trials provide no consistent evidence for nonmusical cognitive benefits of brief preschool music enrichment.

136. Dumont, E., Syurina, E. V., Feron F. J. M. and van Hooren, S. (2017) 'Music interventions and child development: A critical review and further directions', *Frontiers in Psychology* 8 p. 694.

137. Sala, G. and Gobet, F. (2017) 'When the music's over. Does music skill transfer to children's and young adolescents' cognitive and academic skills? A meta-analysis', *Educational Research Review* 20 pp. 55-67.

138. Swaminathan, S., Schellenberg, E. G. and Venkatesan, K. (2018) 'Explaining the association between music training and reading in adults', *Journal of Experimental Psychology: Learning, Memory, and Cognition* 44 (6) pp. 992-999.

139. Rickard, N. S., Bambrick, C. J. and Gill, A. (2012) 'Absence of widespread psychosocial and cognitive effects of school-based music instruction in 10-13-year-old students', *International Journal of Music Education* 30 pp. 57-78.

140. Tervaniemi, M., Tao, S. and Huotilainen, M. (2018) 'Promises of music in education?', *Frontiers of Education* 3 p. 74.

141. Cogo-Moreira, H., Andriolo, R. B., Yazigi, L, Ploubidis, G. B., Brandão de Ávila, C. R. and Mari, J. J. (2012) 'Music education for improving reading skills in children and adolescents with dyslexia', *Cochrane Database of Systematic Reviews* 8.

142. Mostert, M. P. (1999-2000) 'A partial etiology of discriminative disability: Bandwagons and beliefs', *Exceptionality* 8 pp. 117-132.

143. Papadatou-Pastou, M., Haliou, E. and Vlachos, F. (2017) 'Brain knowledge and the prevalence of neuromyths among prospective teachers in Greece', *Frontiers of Psychology* 8 p. 804.

ASSESSING LITERACY SKILLS – PURPOSES, PRACTICALITIES AND PITFALLS

BY JESSIE RICKETTS AND JAMES MURPHY

Despite the frequently expressed concerns about over-testing in the education system, there is a surprising lack of detailed assessment in schools with regard to the fundamentals of literacy competency. Indeed, many teachers are not clear either on what these competencies are, how they should be distinguished, how they should be assessed and how they should be taught.

This chapter outlines the key principles of standardised assessment, and the ways in which standardised assessments can be used constructively to assist the teaching and support of students' literacy, especially for those who struggle. It also warns against over-reliance on standardised tests: such tools are best used as starting points for investigation, rather than as an end in themselves.

Author bio-sketch:

Dr Jessie Ricketts is a Reader (Associate Professor) in the Department of Psychology, Royal Holloway, University of London. Jessie's research has focused on how learning to read and frequent reading benefits children's learning and language. She also works on language and literacy assessment, and has contributed to the development of a number of published assessments. Throughout her career, Jessie has worked closely with teachers to consider issues around assessment and modify her research to maximise its utility for teaching practice. Jessie is a board member for the Society for Scientific Study of Reading and writes a monthly blog for the Times Educational Supplement.

James Murphy has been an English teacher, head of English and senior leader in New Zealand and England. He has a background in special education, education research and literacy. With Dianne Murphy he leads Thinking Reading, working around the UK to help schools deliver a high-impact reading intervention which enables struggling readers at secondary school to catch up completely. He is the co-author of *Thinking Reading: What every secondary teacher needs to know about reading*, published by John Catt Educational, and the editor of *The researchED guide to literacy*.

Why is literacy assessment so important?

If we want to all our students to achieve success with reading and writing, teachers need to have an accurate understanding of pupils' current skill levels. Only then can we plan and teach – and where necessary, intervene – appropriately. Given that literacy skills (such as being able to read accurately and with comprehension, and being able to write connected texts) are foundational to learning and to demonstrating achievement, it is essential that these foundational skills are assessed regularly, accurately and reliably.

As pupils move up the school system, accessing the full curriculum increasingly relies on independent reading. Writing is also key to developing understanding of curriculum topics and demonstrating knowledge, both in the classroom and in school exams. However, reading and writing skills are extremely variable amongst pupils in school.[1,2] For example, in a class of 12 year olds, reading can vary from being able to read only words and sentences, to being able to read at adult-like levels.[3] This variability requires strong and reliable assessment systems to ensure that no students fall through the cracks, and all are given the help that they need. Three important ways in which literacy assessment underpins sound educational practice are:

- to capture variation in classes and identify pupils with literacy needs.
- to target any class-wide instruction or intervention in line with pupils' needs.
- to monitor progress following instruction and intervention.

It is also important to acknowledge the frequently voiced concerns about 'over-testing' within the UK educational system, with many arguing that existing assessments place undue stress and demands on pupils, teachers and schools.[4] These concerns tend to refer to national assessments imposed within England by the

Department for Education, in particular assessments at the end of primary school (Key Stage 2 SATs) and compulsory full-time education (GCSEs). It is important, therefore, that the purpose of additional assessments is clearly related to the reasons outlined above, and not seen as a 'ranking exercise' for students, teachers or schools.

Which students need literacy assessment?

Literacy is a clear focus in the primary school curriculum, particularly early on when there tends to be regular assessment of reading, writing and spelling skills by teachers. In the UK, national assessments include checking students' phonics knowledge early in primary school: through to national assessments of broader reading and writing skills at the end of Year 6. In addition, many schools employ standardised assessments to supplement other assessments. However, increasingly less emphasis is placed on foundational literacy skills as pupils move through primary school and into secondary school. At secondary school this lack of information is stark, with many teachers saying that they do not understand how literacy skills develop and how they can be supported. Typically, foundational literacy support is not considered to be part of their role. Further, they do not receive the training on this that primary teachers experience. Yet, more than 15% of adolescents reach the end of secondary school without the basic literacy skills that are needed for everyday life.[5] Thus, there is clearly a need to continue to assess and support foundational literacy skills beyond primary school.

In this chapter, we outline:

1. the links between theoretical understandings of reading and the nature of effective assessment.
2. the uses and limitations of standardised assessments.
3. practical steps for screening reading and writing skills, particularly in secondary schools.

What can literacy theories tell us about assessment?

Research has provided a number of theoretical frameworks that help us to understand what should be assessed in relation to literacy. Perhaps most influential is the Simple View of Reading (SVR).[6] According to this framework, successful reading – that is, reading accurately and with comprehension – is the product of being able to read words and being able to understand language. The SVR describes reading as a product because both of these sets of skills are necessary for skilled reading, and neither is sufficient on its own.

The SVR can be presented in multi-dimensional space (see Figure 1). This is helpful in explaining individual differences in reading. For most children, word reading and language comprehension processes are correlated, so they vary from being generally poor readers (bottom left quadrant) to being generally good readers (top right quadrant). However, reading skills do dissociate with some children experiencing word reading difficulties in the absence of language comprehension difficulties (top left quadrant), and others experiencing language comprehension difficulties but no difficulty reading words accurately (bottom right quadrant).

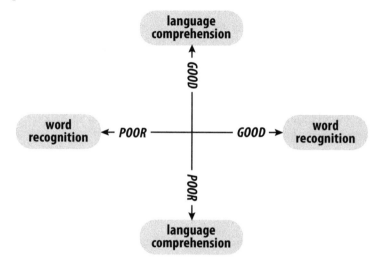

Figure 1. The Simple View of Reading (Tunmer & Gough, 1986)

For every teacher, it is important to know that these different reading profiles likely occur in any classroom. The SVR suggests that if there are concerns about reading, both word reading and language comprehension should be assessed to find out whether these concerns are justified, and if so, where a pupil's needs lie. Such assessment will identify the range of abilities, and identify any pupils who need intervention to promote word reading, language comprehension, or both. Then, further assessments can be put in place to monitor progress in both word reading and language comprehension, as well as in reading comprehension. It is important to note that the relative contribution of word reading and language comprehension to reading success changes with reading progress. Early on, word reading is the primary barrier but for most readers, with a few years of experience, the primary determinant of reading success shifts to language comprehension.

The SVR does not encompass every factor that contributes to reading success (e.g. opportunity to read and motivation). Nonetheless, it is extremely well supported by research evidence.[7] Building on this, the Reading Systems Framework[8] (Perfetti and Stafura, 2014) highlights the aspects of word reading and language comprehension that will be important and how these processes interact so that the reader can build a mental model of the text.

Nation (2019) has proposed an expanded Simple View of Reading (Figure 2) that captures this, as well as the reciprocal nature of the relationship between reading and language. Once children can read, the relationship between reading and spoken language reading provides opportunities for language learning.

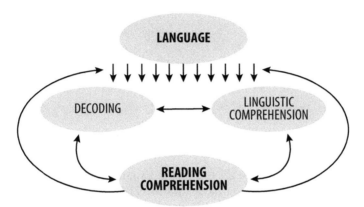

Figure 2. The expanded Simple View of Reading (Nation, 2019)

The discussion so far has focused more on reading than writing. This does not reflect importance: writing is, of course, vital for learning and demonstrating knowledge and skill. However, writing has attracted far less research attention. That said, the Simple View of Writing[9, 10] (Figure 3) provides a useful framework for understanding writing. This view emphasises transcription (handwriting, typing and spelling), text generation (e.g. ideas and language) and executive functions (e.g. planning and working memory). The Simple View of Writing parallels the Simple View of Reading in emphasising the mechanics of literacy, namely word reading or decoding for reading, and spelling and handwriting for writing; it also distinguishes these from other crucial higher level processes (e.g. language). For both reading and writing, these 'Simple Views' do not capture fully the complexity of literacy, but rather identify the most important domains for functional literacy. Simple View of Writing components should be taken into account when assessing writing, so that we can consider variations within a class, identify pupils with literacy needs, target instruction and intervention, and monitor progress.

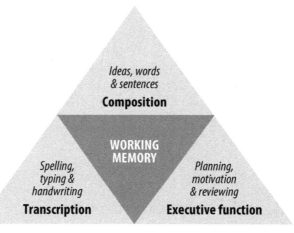

Figure 3. The Simple View of Writing

Practical implications: Assessing reading in schools
What do we need to assess?

So far we have seen that there are two major domains of reading: **decoding** (i.e. deciphering written words accurately and mentally mapping them to spoken words) and **language comprehension** (i.e. how well students can understand the language that is being used in the text).

Decoding skills can be grouped into three main areas:

- Phonological knowledge (being able to discriminate the different sounds in speech)
- Decoding knowledge (accuracy in recognising the appropriate sounds for given spellings and blend so that words can be sounded out)
- Fluency (being able to process the recognition of sound-spellings into familiar spoken words quickly and automatically)

Comprehension consists of a range of sub-domains, including:

- Concepts about text types (for example, genre)
- Vocabulary (which words the student understands and can use accurately)
- Background knowledge (how familiar the child is with the topic)

- Semantics (different ways that meaning is expressed or implied, such as symbolism, imagery and connotations)
- Syntax (how word parts and word order alter meaning and emphasis)
- Discourse processes such as comprehension monitoring and making inferences[8, 11]

How is reading assessed in schools?

The nature of national assessments varies widely. In the UK, two important national assessments of children's reading are the Year 1 Phonics Check, and Key Stage Two SATs assessment (in Year 6). The respective focuses of these two assessments help to illustrate the practical implications of assessing both decoding and comprehension skills.

The Year 1 Phonics Check[12]

In Year 1 (and for some children Year 2), a phonics screening check is administered one-to-one in under ten minutes, using children's reading of 20 words and 20 non-words which between them exemplify the most common elements of the English written code. Test administrators are required to make it clear to pupils whether the words are 'real' words or names for imaginary creatures.

One question frequently raised about this test is: why does it include non-words? Shouldn't children only be assessed on reading real words? The reason for including non-words is that we are assessing not the reading of words, but the sound-spelling correspondences that make up those words. Some children learn to memorise whole words by their shape – in other words, by how they look and not by how they are sounded out. Employing non-words allows us to check that they can decode unfamiliar words, which they cannot have memorised. So why is it so important to check that children can decode early in their education? In English, letters code for sounds, and these letter-sound mappings are mostly systematic. Children who have 'cracked this code' have the tools that they need to learn to read words independently.[13, 14] This is crucial as even the most ambitious curriculum cannot explicitly teach children to read all of the words that they need to know. Some children will learn to decode irrespective of the teaching that they receive, but other children benefit from being taught the code, rather than having to work it out for themselves.

The Year 1 Phonics Check (which is administered again in Year 2 for those who scored below the 'pass' mark in Year 1) enables teachers to identify those students who need additional help with acquiring phonic knowledge. For most children, it will probably be the last time that decoding will be formally assessed in their education. Even in the Key Stage 1 SATs papers, which children sit at the end of Year 2, there is no explicit decoding element.[15]

Year 6 SATs

The Year 6 SATs exams[16] have a controversial history, which there is not space to go into here. Instead let us summarise by saying that students sit externally marked tests in reading; spelling, punctuation and grammar; and, mathematics. The students' scores are scaled against an expected score or 'standard' agreed upon by teaching practitioners. Students who meet the 'expected standard' are considered 'secondary ready' – that is, they are understood to have acquired sufficient skills to be able to access the secondary curriculum.

A number of issues could be debated around this battery of tests, but for now, let us focus on the reading test. This is a written test of a student's reading comprehension. In contrast to the 'phonics only' approach at the end of Year 1, we now have a 'comprehension only' approach at the end of Year 6. Referring back to our earlier discussion of the Simple View of Reading, this test cannot provide a complete picture of students' reading strengths and weaknesses, because it only assess one of the two major domains of reading skills.

One reason that many students are able to reach secondary school with difficulties in reading is the lack of continued assessment of decoding skills at primary school. Add to this number the students whose decoding is reasonable, but whose comprehension skills are weak, and we have a cohort consisting of about 20% beginning secondary school each year with reading below the expected standard.[17, 18] The question naturally arises: what do we do with them?

Pro-active assessment systems

The answer is to ensure that students are pro-actively assessed, starting with the standardised tools that we have available, to ensure that all those with weaknesses are identified early on. While this principle obviously applies to secondary schools, there is every reason to apply this in the primary school setting as well. Some schools rely on referrals from classroom teachers, or simply select children for extra help based on whether they have a formal classification of special educational needs. These pathways are potentially hit and miss, and risk children 'falling through the cracks' so that their needs are not addressed promptly. This can cause them to fall further behind than they needed to, damaging their confidence and self-esteem as learners.[19]

Why are standardised assessments useful?

Standardised assessments can complement other assessments as they can be used to measure specific skills. For example, success on the reading component of the Key Stage 2 SATs test at the end of primary school in England is dependent on many things: being able to read words and texts, vocabulary knowledge, using comprehension processes like making inferences and so on. Standardised tests allow us to isolate these different processes so that we can identify which aspects of reading the pupil is finding difficult.

Standardised tests are developed carefully to ensure that they are:

i. valid, i.e. they measure the skill that they purport to measure.

ii. reliable, such that they would indicate the same conclusion in another situation or on another day.

They are standard in two ways. First, their materials and the way in which they are administered and scored is standard, so that every pupil has the same opportunity to show their knowledge and skills. The same instructions and materials are delivered as similarly as possible.

The second way in which they are standard is that we know what 'standard' or average performance would look like. During the development of a standardised assessment, the task is administered to a large number of children (often thousands) who are representative of a population: share the proportion of children from different ethnic backgrounds, for example. This 'standardisation' or 'normative' sample can then be divided into age bands and their data used to determine, for each age group, what an average score would be, and what the typical variation around that score should be. These calculations are then used to develop normative scores that reflect the average for an age group (the mean) and the average range (within one standard deviation of the mean). This enables us to compare a student's performance to what a 'typical' performance for their age would look like.

There are different types of normative scores. One example of a normative score is a percentile ranking. These are reasonably easy to understand as a child who is 'on the 50th percentile' is average, 50% of their same-age peers should be below this, and 50% above. 'Standard scores' are most commonly used in research and clinical practice, and are reasonably familiar because this is how IQ scores are represented.

A child whose standard score is 100 is average. The standard deviation for this score is 15, so the average range is 85-115. What this means is that children who receive a standard score of 85 or below are performing at a level that is lower than the average range; such a score could indicate that these children might be a cause for concern and might need additional support in order to overcome their difficulties.

Many standardised tests also publish age equivalents, like a reading age. 'Reading ages' are very commonly used to describe performance, because they can seem intuitive. However, using these to identify needs can be very misleading because reading develops at different rates especially in the first few years of instruction. Consider, for example, two children in England who receive a reading age that is seven months below their chronological age. The first child is five years and six months old, and started formal literacy instruction at four years old. In real terms, this child can recognise some letters and can only read a few high frequency words, which is significantly less than most of her same-age peers. Her standard score would be below average, i.e. below 85, and therefore would give cause for concern. The second child is ten years old, and can read texts accurately and with comprehension. Some classmates show better reading, but this child's reading level is not unusual at this age. Parents of both children might be alarmed by their reading ages, but standard scores would reveal that there is only cause for concern for the younger child.

Using standardised tests to screen for literacy problems

Screening to identify children with literacy difficulties (and those whose achievement is exceptionally high) should begin with valid, reliable standardised assessments, and should address the domains of both decoding and comprehension. There are a number of tests that can do this, but few which cover both domains, can be administered to groups, and are normed up to 16 years (the end of secondary schooling in the UK).

As discussed earlier in this chapter, a standard age score below 85 is one standard deviation below the mean. This equates to an age percentile score which would indicate that the student is distinctly 'below average'. However, there are two important points to keep in mind when interpreting standardised scores with an individual student in mind.

The first point is that all standardised tests have a 'standard error of measurement' where they take into account the fact that a specific individual's response to the specific test items on a specific day will be variable, and might have been higher or lower. This potential range is expressed by a 'confidence interval', which is the range of scores within which a student's 'true' score lies, usually at a probability of 90%. For example, let us say that a student achieves a standard score of 80 – well below the mean of 100. However, what this score actually means is that we can be 90% confident that the student's score lies somewhere between 75 (indicating a need for additional support) and 90 (well within the average range, and not requiring support). Given this possible range, the standardised test can only be a starting point. We will need to validate the results more precisely if we want to be able to support the right students with the right kind of help.

The second point is that student motivation can have a significant effect on test scores, particularly for older students. Tests need to be managed very carefully according to the standardisation of administration we discussed above. Even so, a test administered to a group is difficult to run in such a way that we can be sure that every student did their best. Across a large sample – for example, an entire year group – a few low scores will have little impact on our assessment of the cohort as a whole. However, on the individual level, the consequences of a low score may be quite significant, including withdrawal from lessons and the provision of additional literacy support. Therefore, we need to be sure that low scores are not the by-products of low test motivation before we begin to respond.

One way of doing this is to re-test students with a low score. In practical terms, taking into account confidence intervals, this means re-testing those who score in the lowest 35 percentiles, using a similar standardised test. If the student's score is very similar, or lower, we can be more confident that there is a problem. If their score goes up significantly, they can be excluded from the need for further intervention. This procedure requires time at the beginning of the process, but is remarkably effective at screening out students who scored poorly, who do not actually need additional help. This also saves time and money later on.

Close individual assessment

What both of the points above imply is that we are still going to need a third step, where we assess students individually, with a test that employs both phonics and language comprehension components, to determine the specific domains of difficulty and to observe the child's test motivation closely. At this stage it is likely that – particularly with older readers – we will continue to find some students who can do much better than their initial standardised test score indicated. These students too can be screened out, so that we are left with an even smaller pool of students who genuinely need help.

A proactive screening system as described above can be used to ensure that:

1. We can be confident that the students we have identified for extra help really do need it.
2. Students who do not need additional support have been screened out, saving valuable curriculum time as well as staffing resources.
3. Students can now be matched correctly to the kind of intervention they need, depending on whether their needs fall into the decoding or comprehension domains (or both).

4. Resources are targeted more efficiently.

Assessing writing in schools

The business of assessing student writing is similar to that of reading, insofar as the mechanics of writing are being developed at primary school, and the utilisation of these competencies to serve 'higher order' skills is increasingly extended at secondary school. In addition to the accuracy of a student's use of literacy conventions – spelling, punctuation and grammar – there are matters of content, structure, imagery, allusion, concision, clarity and style – to name but a few elements of writing. The principles of standardised assessment as outlined above with respect to reading, are equally applicable to writing. Assessing the full range of aspects of writing is beyond the scope or space of this short article. In terms of the definition of literacy outlined in the introduction, it is most appropriate to focus on the three sets of conventions that form the basis upon which other features are built: spelling, punctuation and grammar.

One practical way in which students can be assessed using a standard format, (without standardised scores) is described below:

> An example is the use of a simple ten-minute writing sample, administered under standard but easily replicable conditions. One way of doing this is for each English teacher to make this one of the first activities of the school year. Introducing herself, she can tell the students that they are going to introduce themselves to her by writing a letter. The teacher brainstorms with the students all the different topics they could write about to describe themselves – family, friends, their neighbourhood, pets, hobbies, sports, books, films, food and so on. The teacher then issues lined paper, and tells students that for this exercise they are going to take just ten minutes. 'I will tell you when you have two minutes and one minute left. Don't worry about correcting any spelling or punctuation errors – I will give you an extra two minutes once we stop writing to check your work and make any corrections that are needed.' The teacher takes questions and checks with individual students to ensure they are clear on the task, then times the group for ten minutes, with a time announcement at eight and nine minutes respectively. The teacher gives students two minutes to identify any errors by circling them (not erasing them), and correcting as many as they have time for. Finally, the teacher asks students to count the number of words they wrote and to write this number at the lower right of the page, with a circle around the number.

Although this is a simple procedure, it has many advantages. First, it is contextual. Students have a pragmatic reason for engaging, i.e. they are indeed introducing themselves to the teacher. Secondly, they have also contributed to the ideas for writing and have already been primed for the exercise. This ensures that there is no 'artificial ceiling' effect where students do not show their writing ability because they were stuck for ideas. Thirdly, the conditions are standardised, which means that the work students produce across the cohort is comparable. Further, the teacher now has a great deal of baseline information about students' spelling, punctuation, grammar, vocabulary, handwriting and writing speed.[20]

The most immediate tasks for using this baseline data are to:

- identify those who produced limited and/or poor quality work.
- collate these results in order to prioritise those students who need help most urgently.
- identify the writing skills in which students will need support.

Summary

Assessing students' literacy ability (not potential) is of the highest importance. Teachers need to understand not only what they need to teach their students, but also to identify those students who may need additional help and support to overcome difficulties. Such screening systems should take account of the research on how we learn to read, ensuring that the domains of both decoding and language comprehension are assessed, and this process should occur earlier rather than later. Delays in identifying students with literacy difficulties can lead to collateral damage in curriculum learning, behaviour, confidence and self-esteem. Even where it is more difficult to apply the principles of standardised testing, for example in the domain of writing, standardised formats can still enable us to derive useful and practical information. Once screening has reliably identified students who need additional help, we should employ close assessment of individual students to find out exactly where their difficulties lie, and then match them closely to well designed, carefully focused interventions.

References

1. Lervåg, A., Melby-Lervåg, M. and Hulme, C. (2018) 'Unpicking the developmental relationships between oral language skills and reading comprehension: It's simple, but complex', *Child development* 89 (5) pp. 1821-1838.

2. Dockrell, J. E., Connelly, V., Walter, K. and Critten, S. (2015) 'Assessing children's writing products: the role of curriculum based measures', *British Educational Research Journal* 41 (4) pp. 575-595.

3. Ricketts, J., Dawson, N., Taylor, L., Lervåg, A. and Hulme, C. (under revision) 'Reading and oral vocabulary and development in early adolescence'.

4. Moran, L. (2019) 'To the children who are sitting SATs this week I know you can do it – but I've no idea why this government is making you', *The Independent* [Online], 19 May. Retrieved from: www.bit.ly/2ouQBq6

5. Jerrim, J. and Shure, N. (2016) *Achievement of 15-Year-Olds in England: PISA 2015 National Report.* Department for Education. London: The Stationery Office.

6. Gough, P. B. and Tunmer, W. E. (1986) 'Decoding, reading, and reading disability', *Remedial and Special Education* 7 (1) pp. 6-10.

7. Ibid (n 1)

8. Perfetti, C. and Stafura, J. (2014) 'Word Knowledge in a Theory of Reading Comprehension', *Scientific Studies of Reading* 18 (1) pp. 22-37.

9. Berninger, V. W., Vaughan, K., Abbott, R. D., Begay, K., Coleman, K. B., Curtin, G., Hawkins, J., M. and Graham, S. (2002) 'Teaching spelling and composition alone and together: Implications for the simple view of writing', *Journal of Educational Psychology* 94 (2) pp. 291-304.

10. Education Endowment Foundation (2018) *Improving Literacy in Key Stage 1: Eight recommendations to support the literacy of 5-7 year-olds.* Retrieved from: www.bit.ly/2plLIjG

11. Scarborough, H. S. (2001) 'Connecting early language and literacy to later reading (dis)abilities: Evidence, theory, and practice' in Neuman, S. and Dickinson, D. (eds) *Handbook for research in early literacy.* New York, NY: Guilford Press, pp. 97-110.

12. Department for Education (2019) *Year 1 Phonics Check: Administration guidance.* Retrieved from: www.bit.ly/2nEQLLK

13. Willingham, D. T. (2017) *The Reading Mind: A Cognitive Approach to Understanding How the Mind Reads.* San Francisco: Jossey-Bass.

14. Ibid.

15. Department for Education (2019) *Key Stage 2: Test administration guidance.* Retrieved from: www.bit.ly/2ouRMG2

16. Ibid.

17. Save the Children (2014) *How reading can help children escape poverty.* Save the Children on behalf of the Read On. Get On. campaign. Retrieved from: www.bit.ly/2mZgQVo

18. Ricketts, J., Dawson, N., Taylor, L., Lervåg, A., & Hulme, C. (under revision) *Reading and oral vocabulary development in early adolescence.*

19. Murphy, D. and Murphy, J. (2018) Thinking Reading: What every secondary teacher needs to know about reading. Woodbridge: John Catt Educational.

20. Ibid (n 19)

A NON-CATEGORICAL APPROACH TO TEACHING LOW-PROGRESS READERS IN THE PRIMARY SCHOOL

BY KEVIN WHELDALL, ROBYN WHELDALL AND JENNIFER BUCKINGHAM

Assessment can tell us that a student is having difficulties. But how do we know why they are struggling? How can we best support them? And what kinds of change can we expect to see – aren't there some children who will never quite 'get it'? In this chapter, three formidable researchers and practitioners in the field of reading intervention join forces to elucidate the potential causes of reading difficulties, and to outline what constitutes effective intervention. They also explain the Response To Intervention framework for escalating the level of intervention that children receive over time, so that everyone gets the help that they need. The story of how evidence-based practice can change children's outcomes is a hopeful one for teachers and their charges; this chapter shows that there is much that can be done.

Author bio-sketch:

Kevin Wheldall AM is an Emeritus Professor of Macquarie University and Chairman of MultiLit Pty Ltd. Having spent nearly 50 years researching and writing in educational psychology and special education, Kevin is recognised internationally as a leading authority in reading assessment and instruction and in classroom behaviour management. Director of Macquarie University Special Education Centre (MUSEC) for over 20 years, he is now an Emeritus Professor of Macquarie University and Chairman of MultiLit Pty Ltd. Kevin is the author of over 300 academic books, chapters and journal articles. His academic standing is recognised by his Fellowship of the prestigious Academy of

Social Sciences in Australia, the British Psychological Society, the College of Preceptors, the College of Educational and Child Psychologists of the Australian Psychological Society and the International Academy for Research in Learning Disabilities. In 2011 he was made a Member (AM) in the Order of Australia for his services to education. For many years, he has consulted to government and other agencies at both federal and state levels.

Dr Robyn Wheldall is a Director of MultiLit Pty Ltd and an Honorary Research Fellow of Macquarie University. Robyn has expertise in researching reading interventions and has worked in the areas of learning difficulties, special education, behaviour management and literacy instruction and interventions for struggling readers for 30 years. She was the Research and Development Manager at MUSEC during the formative years of MultiLit and is a Founding Director of MultiLit Pty Ltd. She has also been the Deputy Director of the MRU since its inception in 2006. She has numerous research publications and extensive project management experience in establishing intensive literacy interventions in school, clinical and community settings. She is currently on the Council of Learning Difficulties Australia, is a Founding Director of the Institute of Special Educators (InSpEd), is on the Industry Advisory Board of the Graduate School of Speech Pathology at UTS, is the Co-Editor of Nomanis and is an Honorary Research Fellow of Macquarie University from whom she has received a Community Outreach Award for her MultiLit work.

Dr Jennifer Buckingham is Director of Strategy, MultiLit Pty Ltd and the Five from Five Project and Senior Research Fellow at the MultiLit Research Unit. Jennifer is the Founder of the Five from Five project which provides evidence-based information on effective reading instruction. Her PhD research was on effective instruction for struggling readers. She has provided advice on reading instruction and policy to the NSW, Victorian, South Australian and federal governments and was the chair of the expert advisory group to the federal government on a Year 1 literacy and numeracy assessment. Jennifer is a board member of the Australian Institute for Teaching and School Leadership.

Literacy is unquestionably at a premium. It is increasingly difficult to gain employment in the 21st century without having first acquired, at the very least, basic functional literacy. Most of the manual labouring jobs of the past that required little or no literacy skill to perform them satisfactorily have become obsolete, first with increasing mechanisation and automation, and latterly with the near universal application of information technology (IT) to employment related, as well as social and recreational, activities. It is now clear that the advent of IT into all spheres of human activity requires greater literacy skill, not less, and from a far wider spectrum within the population. Someone who struggles to read and spell is severely disadvantaged in such an environment. Consequently, proficiency in reading and spelling has never been such a priority as it is today.

Given these considerations, it is particularly disturbing to find that unacceptably large proportions of the population still struggle with reading and writing, as recent surveys have repeatedly shown.[1] That there is a significantly large minority of the population who continue to struggle in this way is a cause for shame.

In this chapter, we shall discuss how best to ensure that the vast majority of children leave primary school able to read accurately and fluently and to understand what they read. Our arguments are predicated on a basic understanding of the scientific evidence and theory of how children learn to read including the 'Five Big Ideas' and the 'Simple View of Reading'. These ideas have already been introduced in Chapter 3 and hence we shall not repeat them here, taking time only to emphasise that these models of how reading works and is learnt underpin all instruction – both initial and remedial instruction.

Why do so many children struggle to learn to read?

Students struggle to learn to read for a variety of reasons. The actual causes of reading disability are frequently not known, are more often hypothesised than proven, and tend to be inferred from the fact that such students are failing to progress at the same rate as their peers. This is one reason why we prefer to use the more neutral, generic term 'low-progress readers'.

As a result of scientific research carried out over the past 40 years or so, most reading scientists now subscribe to variations of the phonological-deficit theory of reading difficulties, that is that reading problems are largely the result of language difficulties, specifically the ability to segment and to blend the component sounds within words.[2] Problems in phonological processing may arise from: **intrinsic**, often heritable, phonological processing difficulties; **extrinsic** difficulties resulting from an impoverished language and literacy learning environment; or both.[3]

It is important to emphasise that intrinsic and extrinsic factors are probably both differentially distributed. The practical import of this is that even students whose inherent phonological processing ability is somewhat reduced as a result of intrinsic (biological) factors, but whose performance is extraordinarily low because they have suffered the 'double whammy' of this being coupled with a poor literacy learning environment (at home and/or school), can be helped once effective instruction is provided. On the other hand, students who have enjoyed an optimal language and literacy learning environment, but whose intrinsic phonological processing ability is severely compromised, are probably still going to struggle even when provided with exemplary, evidence-based best practice remedial instruction, and are likely to need continuing support over many years (see diagram below).[4]

	Phonological Ability (PA)			
		High	Average	Low
	High	High progress readers	Above average readers	Hidden and classic dyslexic readers
	Average	Above average readers	Average readers	Regular dyslexic readers
Quality of Literacy Learning Environment (QLLE)	Low	Below average readers	Below average readers	Doubly disadvantaged dyslexic readers

The Simple View of Reading (see Chapter 3) tells us that language comprehension is also a factor. Together, word decoding and language comprehension predict between 95% and 99% of variation in reading comprehension.[5, 6] The remaining variance is plausibly explained by measurement error (either statistical or assessment precision).[7]

Language comprehension is more heavily predicted by environmental factors – both at home and at school – which might suggest it would be more amenable to remediation by instruction. However, the cumulative nature of language competency, especially vocabulary, makes language comprehension more susceptible to 'Matthew effects' and, therefore, it is more difficult to close the gaps.[8] Children who begin school with language comprehension deficits tend to fall increasingly further behind their peers, whose language competency accelerates when they begin independent reading.

Theoretically, this is all very interesting but does it actually help us much in practice?

Diagnosis

Endemic within the field of research and practice in reading disability has been a preoccupation with the diagnosis of the underlying causes of reading difficulties, specifically to identify those students who may be said to be dyslexic as against being the so-called 'garden variety' low-progress readers.[9] In some countries, a formal diagnosis of a learning disability such as dyslexia may make access more likely to increased facilities and support, curricular and assessment dispensations, and, not least, special funding. Until recent years, the most widely accepted definition and diagnosis of dyslexia was predicated upon an observed discrepancy between a child's reading performance and his/her more general intellectual and/or verbal ability. This 'discrepancy' model has been discredited and is currently being largely replaced by the *Response to Intervention* (RtI) model, to which we shall return.[10, 11]

But there is a more fundamental objection to this preoccupation with diagnosis and categorisation, regardless of how or whether the categories may be substantiated objectively. While the label of dyslexia, or learning disability more generally, may afford some comfort to students struggling to read and to their parents, in our present state of knowledge, at least, there are few if any implications of such a diagnosis for specific instructional intervention that is any different from what we might offer any student struggling to learn to read. Some of the loose talk surrounding diagnosis and remediation of dyslexia presupposes a magic bullet to fix the reading disability specifically of children with dyslexia, access to which they will somehow be denied without an appropriate diagnosis. But the form of instruction we should offer should be no different from that which we would offer to any struggling reader and this form of instruction should be predicated upon evidence-based best practice as identified by scientific research into effective instruction in reading and related skills.

In spite of considerable research into so-called 'aptitude-treatment interactions' there is no convincing body of evidence to suggest that students with different disabling conditions need different forms of instruction;[12] rather, it appears that effective instruction for struggling readers is effective instruction generally.

A non-categorical approach

It is for this reason that we, among many scientifically-orientated reading researchers and practitioners these days, subscribe to what is known as a 'non-categorical approach' to teaching students with learning difficulties in the area of literacy.[13, 14] Quite simply, knowing whether a child is dyslexic or not, or the reason why she or he has struggled to learn to read, offers no help in determining what to do to help him or her to master the skills necessary for reading and spelling. Consequently, it makes more sense to address the problem of poor reading directly, regardless of the hypothesised causation, using the most powerful instructional interventions that have been shown to be effective.

So what does this mean for practice? It requires us to focus on the *solution* not the cause. A careful needs-based appraisal of the student's current level of performance in a skill area (a curriculum-based assessment) will help us to determine the entry point for instruction and to decide on the method or programme to be employed. This is not necessarily to say that 'one size fits all' – there may be several alternative instructional programmes that have been shown to be effective but the selection of the most appropriate programme will be determined by the idiosyncratic needs of the individual child and his or her responsiveness to instruction, not the category of his or her disabling condition.[15] We like to regard this as a truly child-centred approach to education. A non-categorical approach also aligns very well with the Response to Intervention model, providing a more sound basis for reaching conclusions about the severity of a child's difficulties in mastering reading and spelling skills than the discrepancy models used in the past.

Response to Intervention (RtI)

Response to Intervention (RtI) is a tiered model of instruction for students experiencing difficulties in acquiring basic skills and appropriate social behaviours.[16] Tiered instruction commonly (but not invariably) comprises instruction at three increasing levels of intensity. In the context of literacy instruction, it is predicated upon exemplary initial instruction in reading and related skills being provided at the whole class level during the first few years of schooling. This is known as Tier 1 instruction. Experiencing initial instruction based on evidence-based best practice will ensure that the vast majority of students will get off to a good start in learning to read and spell. Those students who begin to fall behind, often operationally defined as those in the bottom 25% of what might be expected for the age cohort, are then offered Tier 2 instruction.

Tier 2 instruction typically takes the form of more intensive and targeted small group literacy instruction, again based on what scientific research has shown to be the most effective methods and curriculum content for teaching lower-progress readers. Students are taught in small groups of about four students, preferably by a teacher or paraprofessional who is well versed and skilled in the delivery of effective remedial instructional programmes. Such instruction should be provided daily, if possible, for at least half an hour. This more intensive option is reserved for those 'failing to thrive' under the regular classroom regime of Tier 1. Tier 2 level intervention is likely to resolve the difficulties experienced by the great majority of low-progress readers and will enable them to get 'back on track' and progressing at a similar level to their classroom peers.[17, 18] There will always be a few students, however, who fail to respond even when offered this more intensive level of Tier 2 instruction and these students need Tier 3 intervention.

Again, Tier 3 intervention does not necessarily involve appreciably different instruction from that offered in Tier 2 except insofar as the instruction provided is even more intensive, in more specifically targeted form, tailored to the specific needs of the individual student, on a one-to-one basis, and preferably provided by a reading expert.

Within the RtI model, students with a learning disability such as dyslexia may be defined as those students needing continuing intervention, students who are still struggling even when they have been offered both exemplary initial reading instruction (Tier 1), subsequent exemplary small group remedial instruction (Tier 2) and individualised, intensive reading instruction (Tier 3). These are typically the students who are likely to need continuing literacy support, possibly over many years. The pyramid diagram shown below summarises the RtI model. All children need exemplary Tier 1 instruction and this is likely to be sufficient for about 80% of the age cohort to learn to read well. Around 20% of children, however, are likely to fall behind, however, and will need Tier 2 small group instruction to get them back on track. But about 5% of the age cohort will need even more support than this, in the form of intensive individualised instruction – Tier 3. A very small number of children are likely to need this level of support on a continuing basis, for several years.

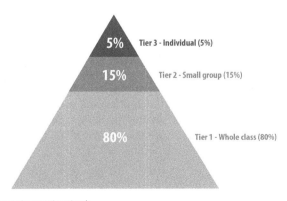

Figure 1. Response to Intervention triangle

Determining the level of instruction required

In our present state of knowledge, we have no way of telling in advance just who will be the students that need Tier 2 and Tier 3 support other than by using the 'suck it and see' approach of RtI coupled with very careful progress monitoring. The question then arises of how best to judge whether a child is responding well to instruction or not and hence whether she or he needs Tier 2 or Tier 3 intervention. Traditional reading tests are of limited use for this purpose since they are not usually sensitive enough to pick up small gains over short periods of time, nor should they be repeated frequently or after only a short time interval, if they are to provide reliable measures. On the other hand, it would not be in the best interests of children to remain for too long on a programme under which they were failing to progress and which will only be detected when they are retested at the end of the year or even after six months.

Progress monitoring using curriculum-based measurement (CBM)

Curriculum-based fluency measures have emerged as the preferred alternative for progress monitoring. Oral reading fluency may be measured by passage reading tests or reading lists of words: having a student read aloud a passage of text or the list of words and counting the number of words read correctly in one minute. This seemingly rather crude index in fact correlates highly with other more complex measures of reading, including both reading accuracy and reading comprehension. Because this exercise may be repeated frequently with different but parallel samples of text from the curriculum at a very similar level of difficulty, this provides a ready means of tracking progress over time. Moreover, these curriculum-based measures are quick and easy to administer.[19, 20]

Curriculum-based measurement (CBM) provides the means by which we can determine the tier of support a student requires. First, a curriculum-based measure may be used as a simple screening instrument to determine which students are struggling to keep up with their peers, say the bottom 25%. (Note that we advocate a slightly higher percentage than is commonly deployed in the RtI model, to allow for measurement error and false positives.) These students are then offered Tier 2 small group remedial instruction. By subsequently monitoring progress on a weekly or fortnightly basis over about six weeks we may then determine who is responding readily and who is not and hence who is likely to need more intensive, individualised Tier 3 instruction for greater and continuing duration, and even whom we might choose to refer to as having 'dyslexia', for administrative/funding purposes. Children who return to regular Tier 1 classroom instruction should ideally continue to be monitored. They may require a further period of Tier 2 intervention if they do not maintain their progress.[21]

Examples of curriculum-based measures of reading include DIBELS,[22] AIMSweb,[23] and the Wheldall Assessment of Reading Passages (WARP).[24]

Thus, it may be seen how a non-categorical approach to remedial instruction for low-progress readers aligns very well with the Response to Intervention model, supported by curriculum-based measurement, and offers the best option for helping all low-progress readers in our present state of knowledge.

What should be taught?

Exemplary instruction, in our view, should necessarily address the Five Big Ideas of reading instruction: phonemic awareness, phonics, fluency, vocabulary and comprehension. While, arguably, phonemic awareness, fluency, vocabulary and comprehension are quite often addressed in many whole language lessons, phonics instruction is often neglected, or taught as a secondary consideration – phonics as the method of last resort. Moreover, when phonics is taught in classrooms it is more likely to be taught as analytic or incidental phonics rather than as systematic, synthetic phonics (SSP). It is little wonder, then, that in some schools (especially those in less advantaged areas), large percentages are found to be in need of Tier 2 provision at the beginning of Year 1; sometimes 50% or more of children are located in the bottom quartile (25%) for reading performance. These children are not necessarily brought up to the level of their peers and so we may see similar percentages at the end of Year 1, in some schools. This has resulted in far too many children who would otherwise have learnt to read with relative ease, failing to do so – the so-called 'instructional casualties'.

If at least 80% of children are not making adequate progress, as the RtI model predicts that they should, then clearly there is something wrong with the Tier 1, universal, whole class provision on offer. It cannot be considered exemplary. The RtI model effectively provides us with a means of judging the adequacy of our Tier 1 instruction.

How should it be taught?

An extensive research literature accumulated over several decades points to explicit and systematic instruction as being the most effective pedagogy for both initial teaching and intervention in reading.[25, 26]

An effective programme of early literacy instruction will have at its core an explicit and systematic phonics component to teach the alphabetic code. This should be included daily for at least 20-30 minutes until the full code has been taught. Well-designed programmes will provide multiple engaging activities within this session to ensure that children's attention is sustained. In addition to phonics instruction (which would also address phonemic awareness and fluency), there should also be an extensive focus on oral language, vocabulary and comprehension using quality children's literature so that all elements of the Five Big Ideas are addressed.[27, 28] InitiaLit is an example of such a programme.[29,30] A wealth of free resources and information on teaching the Five Big Ideas is also available on the Five from Five website.[31]

Explicit instruction is an evidence-based pedagogy in which the teacher:

- explains, models and demonstrates the content or skill to be learnt.
- has a stated learning objective for each lesson.
- uses clear and unambiguous language.
- consistently and cumulatively reviews taught content to ensure retention.
- monitors for understanding.
- provides feedback and correction at the point of need.

Systematic instruction means that there is a planned sequence of phonics elements that comprises a logical progression of skills and knowledge, with sufficient practice and cumulative review for mastery to be achieved. Synthetic phonics is highly explicit and systematic. It is characterised by a number of steps involving grapheme-phoneme correspondence (GPC) (being able to match a phoneme to a grapheme and vice versa).

Early intervention for young struggling readers

Intervention for young struggling readers will generally encompass all of the Five Big Ideas but will almost always focus instruction more heavily on phonological decoding, as this skill is most likely to be constraining their reading comprehension at this stage in their development. Fluent and accurate word and sentence reading is the prerequisite for reading for meaning.

After one year of initial instruction, the performance of all students is screened to identify those students in the bottom quartile of the age cohort, who are struggling to make satisfactory progress. These students are offered Tier 2 supplementary intensive instruction in small groups of no more than four students. Such instruction should be direct, explicit and systematic, again being predicated on the findings from scientific reading research. Most young struggling readers will be helped back on track following Tier 2 intervention leaving only a very small minority – perhaps less than 5% – in need of Tier 3 intervention that comprises even more intensive intervention offered on a one to one basis.

In many western countries, the first line of support for young struggling readers has been, for 30 or more years now, Reading Recovery, a one to one remedial programme. Putting issues of efficacy to one side (but about which we have serious concerns),[32, 33] this is clearly not very cost-effective. Providing one to one intervention from a reading specialist for every young struggling reader is a very expensive option that is simply not viable. It makes good economic sense to offer first an intensive small group intervention because the research evidence shows that most struggling young readers will be helped back on track as a result, leaving a much smaller minority needing individual support.

We have researched and developed such a programme known as 'MiniLit', for example. Meeting Initial Needs In Literacy (MiniLit) is an evidence-based, explicit programme for teaching reading skills to small groups of young children who are at serious risk of falling behind in reading and related skills.[34] It is a Tier 2 intervention programme that provides reading instruction for young struggling readers who have failed to make progress after their first year of formal schooling and is inclusive of the lowest performing students.

Intervention for older low-progress readers

Early intervention in Years 1 and 2 is the preferred method and is likely to be much easier to achieve and more effective than with older primary aged and secondary students. One of the reasons for this is that instruction in basic reading skills is often discontinued from Year 3 on, as the emphasis turns from learning to read to reading to learn. This additional challenge to successful remediation should never mean adopting the attitude that it is too late to help students in the later years of school.

In some respects, intervention with older low-progress readers (children in upper primary and secondary school) should be much the same as for young struggling readers: it should be predicated on a programme that uses the Simple View of Reading and the 'Five Big Ideas' as reference points. Effective interventions for older low progress readers is informed by evidence derived from sound research.[35]

Determining the instructional emphasis of the intervention will depend on identification of the reading subskills that have weaknesses.[36] Most older low-progress readers with low reading comprehension have poor decoding skills and/or poor fluency and will require a strong emphasis on decoding using systematic synthetic phonics instruction. Such instruction will provide them with the foundational word reading accuracy and automaticity that will allow them to concentrate on comprehension when reading.

Older low-progress readers with poor word reading and decoding skills have often learnt unhelpful 'habits' as they have struggled to learn to read, largely because they were taught to read using inefficient and ineffective methods. In 'whole language' or 'balanced literacy' inspired teaching that is advocated in literacy teaching text books, children are urged to use the three cueing systems model.[37] This model comprises in order of importance: contextual (or semantic) cues; syntactical cues; and (last and by all means least) graphophonic cues (letter-sound information). Children are frequently told to 'look at the picture', or asked 'what word would fit in there?' (what Goodman refers to as the 'psycholinguistic guessing game'[38]). When students don't know a word they will frequently look at the teacher for help in the form of one of these prompts. Teaching older low-progress readers to read often involves trying to undo these unhelpful strategies, which can interfere with the more effective methods of systematic synthetic phonics instruction being taught.

Catching older low-progress readers up quickly requires instruction at the point of need. Older students with poor decoding skills are likely to have acquired some letter-sound knowledge and, therefore, an assessment to determine the gaps in their knowledge will be preferable to beginning instruction at the start of a phonics scope and sequence. These students should be provided with decodable books to consolidate their phonic decoding skills. It is important that these be age-appropriate, particularly in secondary school.[39]

However, it should also be noted that not all older low progress readers have weaknesses in word reading or decoding. There is a small proportion (estimated at around 5% of children) who are described in the research literature as 'poor comprehenders'.[40] These children can read aloud a passage of text with an age-appropriate level of accuracy and fluency but demonstrate a poor understanding of what they have read. Therefore, interventions focusing on decoding alone will not be effective as their difficulties are likely be associated with the linguistic or oral language component of the Simple View of Reading model.[41] Language comprehension is a complex activity involving numerous linguistic and cognitive processes. These students may require further assessment to determine the nature of their difficulties.

Vocabulary may be limited, or other specific aspects of reading comprehension such as making inferences and connections may require instructional attention.[42] Tier 2 interventions focused on developing inferencing have been found to be effective in improving comprehension.[43] Instruction based on training in comprehension strategies like summarising can also be helpful but are limited in their effect – more does not necessarily mean better.[44] Sustained improvement will come from developing the foundational skills and knowledge that contribute to reading comprehension.

The 'MacqLit' programme (*Macquarie literacy programme for small group instruction*) has been developed to meet the needs of older low-progress readers.[45] It is an explicit and systematic reading intervention programme for small groups of older low-progress readers specifically aimed at struggling readers in Year 3 and above, the majority of whom need intensive instruction in phonological decoding so they can read fluently. It provides teachers with a comprehensive sequence of lessons that includes all the key components necessary for effective reading instruction.

Conclusions

In this chapter, we have argued that, in some ways, the instruction that needs to be provided to low-progress and struggling readers is no different from the exemplary instruction we should provide to beginning readers. It should be predicated largely on systematic, synthetic phonics instruction. (The 5% of poor comprehenders who can readily decode is an exception.) The critical differences are the intensity and duration of instruction likely to be needed by low-progress readers.

We have also argued against an over-emphasis on diagnosis of reading difficulties in favour of a non-categorical model that focuses upon the individual and idiosyncratic needs of the individual child.

If we are to achieve our goal of ensuring that all (or very nearly all) children learn to read at an acceptable standard by the end of primary school, the Response to Intervention model coupled with a scientific evidence-based approach to effective reading instruction, is our best hope.

References

1. Organisation for Economic Cooperation and Development (2017) *Building skills for all in Australia.* Paris: OECD.

2. Melby-Lervåg, M., Lyster, S. A. and Hulme, C. (2012) 'Phonological skills and their role in learning to read: A meta-analytic review', *Psychological Bulletin* 138 (2) pp. 322-352.

3. Buckingham, J., Beaman, R. and Wheldall, K. (2014) 'Why poor children are more likely to become poor readers: The early years', *Educational Review* 66 (4) pp. 428-446.

4. Wheldall, K. and Beaman, R. (2011) 'Effective instruction for older low-progress readers: Meeting the needs of indigenous students' in Wyatt-Smith, C., Elkins, J. and Gunn, S. (eds) *Multiple perspectives on difficulties in learning literacy and numeracy.* New York, NY: Springer, pp. 255-273.

5. Hjetland, H. N., Lervåg, A., Lyster, S. A. H., Hagtvet, B. E., Hulme, C. and Melby-Lervåg, M. (2019) 'Pathways to reading comprehension: A longitudinal study from 4 to 9 years of age', *Journal of Educational Psychology* 11 (5) pp. 751-763.

6. Lonigan, C. J., Burgess, S. R. and Schatschneider, C. (2018) 'Examining the simple view of reading with elementary school children: Still simple after all these years', *Remedial and Special Education* 39 (5) pp. 260-273.

7. Hoover, W. A. and Tunmer, W. E. (2018) 'The Simple View of Reading: Assessments of its adequacy', *Remedial and Special Education* 39 (5) pp. 304-312.

8. Cain, K. and Oakhill, J. (2011) 'Matthew Effects in young readers: reading comprehension and reading experience aid vocabulary development', *Journal of Learning Disabilities* 44 (5) pp. 431-443.

9. Catts, H. W., Hogan, T. P. and Fey, M. E. (2003) 'Subgrouping poor readers on the basis of individual differences in reading-related abilities', *Journal of Learning Disabilities* 36 (2) pp. 151-164.

10. Siegel, L. S. (1989) 'IQ is irrelevant to the definition of learning disabilities', *Journal of Learning Disabilities* 22 pp. 469-478.

11. Stuebing, K. K., Fletcher, J. M., LeDoux, J. M., Lyon, G. R., Shaywitz, S. E. and Shaywitz, B. A. (2002) 'Validity of IQ-Discrepancy classifications of reading disabilities: A meta-analysis', *American Educational Research Journal* 39 (2) pp. 469-518.

12. Stuebing, K. K., Barth, A. E., Trahan, L. H., Reddy, R. R., Miciak, J. and Fletcher, J. M. (2015) 'Are Child Cognitive Characteristics Strong Predictors of Responses to Intervention? A Meta-Analysis', *Review of Educational Research* 85 (3) pp. 395-429.

13. Wheldall, K. (1994) 'Why do contemporary special educators favour a non-categorical approach to teaching?', *Special Education Perspectives* 3 (1) pp. 45-47.

14. Wheldall, K. and Carter, M. (1996) 'Reconstructing behaviour analysis in education: A revised behavioural interactionist perspective for special education', *Educational Psychology* 16 (2) pp. 121-140.

15. McArthur, G. and Castles, A. (2017) 'Helping children with reading difficulties: Some things we have learned so far', *npj Science of Learning* 2 (7).

16. Fletcher, J. M. and Vaughn, S. (2007) 'Response to Intervention: Preventing and remediating academic difficulties', *Child Development Perspectives* 3 (1) pp. 30-37.

17. Wanzek, J., Vaughn, S., Scammacca, N., Gatlin, B., Walker, M. A. and Capin, P. (2016) 'Meta-analysis of the effects of tier 2 type reading interventions in grades K-3', *Educational Psychology Review* 28 (3) pp. 551-576.

18. Hall, M. S. and Burns, M. K. (2018) 'Meta-analysis of targeted small group reading interventions', *Journal of School Psychology* 66 pp. 54-66.

19. Reynolds, M., Wheldall, K. and Madelaine, A. (2009) 'Building the WARL: The development of the Wheldall Assessment of Reading Lists, a curriculum-based measure designed to identify young struggling readers and monitor their progress', *Australian Journal of Learning Difficulties* 14 pp. 89-111.

20. Reynolds, M., Wheldall, K. and Madelaine, A. (2011) 'Early identification of young struggling readers: Preliminary benchmarks for intervention for students in years one and two in schools in New South Wales', *Australian Journal of Learning Difficulties* 16 (2) pp. 127-143.

21. Stecker, P. M., Fuchs, D. and Fuchs, L. S. (2008) 'Progress Monitoring as Essential Practice within Response to Intervention', *Rural Special Education Quarterly* 27 (4) pp. 10-17.

22. Good, R. H. and Kaminski, R. A. (eds) (2002) *Dynamic Indicators of Basic Early Literacy Skills* (sixth edition). Eugene, OR: Institute for the Development of Educational Achievement.

23. NCS Pearson (2012) *aimsWEB Technical Manual.* Bloomington, MN: NCS Pearson Inc.

24. Wheldall, K. and Madelaine, A. (2013) *The Wheldall assessment of reading passages (WARP) manual.* Sydney: MultiLit Pty Ltd.

25. Castles, A., Rastle, K. and Nation, K. (2018) 'Ending the reading wars: Reading acquisition from novice to expert', *Psychological Science in the Public Interest* 19 (1) pp. 5-51.

26. Stockard, J., Wood, T. W., Coughlin, C and Khoury, C. R. (2017) 'The Effectiveness of Direct Instruction Curricula: A Meta-Analysis of a Half Century of Research', *Review of Educational Research* 88 (4) pp. 479-507.

27. Armbruster, B. B., Lehr, F. and Osborn, J. (2001) *Put reading first: The research building blocks for teaching children to read.* Jessup, MD: National Institute for Literacy.

28. Snow, C. E, Burns, M. S. and Griffin, P. (eds) (1998) *Preventing reading difficulties in young children.* Washington, DC: National Academy Press.

29. MultiLit (2017) *InitiaLit-F: whole class instruction in literacy.* Sydney: MultiLit Pty Ltd.

30. MultiLit (2018) *InitiaLit-1: whole class instruction in literacy.* Sydney: MultiLit Pty Ltd.

31. Reynolds, M. and Wheldall, K. (2007) 'Reading Recovery twenty years down the track: Looking forward, looking back', *International Journal of Disability, Development and Education* 54 (2) pp. 199-223.

32. Ibid (n 20)

33. New South Wales Centre for Education Statistics and Evaluation (2015) *Reading Recovery: A sector-wide analysis.* Sydney: NSW CESE.

34. MultiLit (2011) *MiniLit early literacy intervention program.* Sydney: MultiLit Pty Ltd.

35. Edmonds, M. S., Vaughn, S., Wexler, J., Reutebuch, C., Cable, A., Tackett, K. K. and Schnakenberg, J. W. (2009) 'A synthesis of reading interventions and effects on reading comprehension outcomes for older struggling readers', *Review of Educational Research* 79 (1) pp. 262-300.

36. Snowling, M. and Hulme, C. (2011) 'Evidence-based interventions for reading and language difficulties: creating a virtuous circle', *British Journal of Educational Psychology* 81 (1) pp. 1-23.

37. Buckingham, J. and Meeks, L. (2019) *Short-changed: Preparation to teach reading in initial teacher education.* Sydney: MultiLit Pty Ltd.

38. Goodman, K. S. (1967) 'Reading: A psycholinguistic guessing game', *Journal of the Reading Specialist* 6 (4) pp. 126-135.

39. Murphy, J. and Murphy, D. (2018) *Thinking reading: What every secondary teacher needs to know about reading*. Woodbridge: John Catt Educational.

40. Nation, K. (2019) 'Children's reading difficulties, language, and reflections on the Simple View of Reading', *Australian Journal of Learning Difficulties* 24 (1) pp. 47-73.

41. Spencer, M. and Wagner, R. K. (2018) 'The comprehension problems of children with poor reading comprehension despite adequate decoding: A meta-analysis', *Review of Educational Research* 88 (3) pp. 366-400.

42. Cain, K., Oakhill, J. and Elbro, C. (2014) *Understanding and teaching reading comprehension: A handbook*. Abingdon: Routledge.

43. Elleman, A. M. (2017) 'Examining the impact of inference instruction on the literal and Inferential comprehension of skilled and less skilled readers: A meta-analytic review', *Journal of Educational Psychology* 109 (6) pp. 761-781.

44. Willingham, D. (2006/7) 'The usefulness of brief instruction in reading comprehension strategies', *American Educator*, Winter 2006/7. Retrieved from: www.bit.ly/2mUPqQj

45. MultiLit (2016) *Macquarie literacy program for small group instruction*. Sydney: MultiLit Pty Ltd.

SPELLING: FROM WORDS IN THE HEAD TO WORDS ON THE PAGE

BY RHONA STAINTHORP

Spelling is a topic that puts many of us into a cold sweat. Some of us have never quite mastered it, even if we are good at reading – and some of us struggle with how to teach something that seems to defy logic. Why, for instance, are *strait* and *straight* spelt differently? Why are some words spelt the same way but pronounced differently? Why are there so many possibilities for how a sound may be spelt in English? In this chapter, Professor Rhona Stainthorp, one of our foremost academics in the field, explains many of the puzzling issues around how spelling works – and by implication, how we should teach it. If you have never quite understood why people talk about the importance of phonics, or if you have worried about how to teach spelling, this chapter is a valuable introduction to the topic.

Author bio-sketch:

Rhona Stainthorp is a Professor in the Institute of Education at the University of Reading. She began her working life as a teacher in an all-boys secondary modern school in an outer London borough. Some of her pupils were hardly able to read or write, so she decided to go to Birkbeck College in London to do a further degree in psychology in the hope of learning how to help her pupils. That was 35 years ago. For the rest of her professional life she has worked in higher education departments training teacher and speech and language therapists. Her research has centred on the development of literacy skills: reading, spelling and writing. She is committed to ensuring that teachers are informed about the research evidence that links our understanding the processes involved in learning to read and write and the approach that teachers need to take to ensure their teaching is effective.

The act of spelling is the production of the graphic representations of words in a conventional form. Once people have learnt how to spell this act usually becomes a speedy transcription of the words they wish to produce to create texts: from words in the head to words on the page/screen. This may seem a little tortuous as a definition, but it is important to stress that spelling is not an end in itself. Being able to produce words in an accurate way when writing (i.e. being able to spell them) means that any reader should be able to access the meaning without having to work out which words writers were intending to use. Ability to spell accurately supports people's ability to communicate through the written form. Thus, spelling is a central process of text writing, just as accurate word reading is central to reading comprehension. Spelling is at the service of the text.

It is helpful to begin with a framework in order to contextualise the place of spelling within text writing. A Simple View of Writing[1] (SVW) was proposed, which paralleled the Simple View of Reading[2] (SVR). The SVR proposes that reading is the product of processes that enable the individual words on the page to be identified, and processes that enable the language locked in the words on the page to be understood. According to the SVW, writing is the product of two sets of complex skills: text generation (ideation) and transcription (handwriting/keyboarding and spelling). Text generation involves the generation and organisation of ideas and their translation into internal verbal language, which then has to be transcribed into words on the page. However, this simple view did not capture the complexity of all the processes that have to be orchestrated for writing sufficiently well, so it was expanded into the Not So Simple View [3,4] by the addition of self-regulatory processes and working memory as set out in Figure 1.

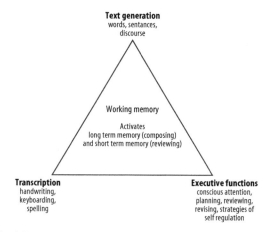

Figure 1. The Not So Simple View

Working memory is conceptualised as being at the centre of the processes because it is needed for accessing long-term memory during the planning and composing phase, and short-term memory is needed during the reviewing phase.[5]

Writing is recognised to be one of the most cognitively demanding tasks humans can engage in.[6] Indeed, ideation (text generation) always remains complex and demanding of cognitive resources. However, the transcription skills are capable of being automated to a great extent and when this happens cognitive resources are freed up for the cognitively demanding text generation processes. This means that by gaining control over transcription the quality of the texts can be improved.[7, 8]

The transcription processes involve language being produced via hand movements to generate the individual words' orthographic identities: their spelling. When texts are created by handwriting, the motor programme involves the production of the letters by scribing. Writers literally produce the words. Writers can also see the text being created as the hand moves across the page so there is a continuous process of reviewing which supports accurate spelling. When the texts are created via a keyboard, writers must recognise where the letters are on the keyboard and then execute a series of key presses in the correct sequence. Depending on the level of touch-typing skill, writers may or may not see the words appearing on the screen individually.

Because this book is written in English, we first need to cover the characteristics of the English spelling system, which is one of the most difficult to learn. Understanding the characteristics of the spelling system, leads to rational approaches to teaching spelling. The very nature of English orthography makes for complications in presenting unambiguous information about spelling without simultaneous audio, so the following conventions are used:

- When letters are being discussed they are presented in angled brackets < >:
  - 'the consonant letter <t>; the vowel letters <oa>.'
- When a word is the item under discussion it is in italics:
  - e.g. '*sit* is made up of the letters <s> <i> <t>.'
- There is not enough space to present a complete account of phonology here, and it would be unreasonable to expect every reader to have expert knowledge of the International Phonetic Alphabet (IPA), which is a system whereby there is a unique unequivocal symbol for every phoneme of all known languages. However, to ensure clarity, when

phonemes are being discussed, the IPA symbols are used between slashes / /, and an exemplification from English words given if necessary:

- e.g. 'the word *sit* is composed of three phonemes, /s/ /ɪ/ /t/ and spelt with the three letters <s> <i> <t>.'
- Some of the IPA symbols are the same as Latin letters and can be used unambiguously for readers of English. However, many phonemes have to be represented by specific IPA symbols:
  - e.g. 'the word *chuck* is composed of three phonemes /tʃ/ /ʌ/ /k/ and spelt with five letters <c> <h> <u> <c> <k>; the phoneme /tʃ/ is represented by the consonant letters <ch>; the phoneme /ʌ/ is represented by the vowel letter <u>; and the phoneme /k/ is represented by the consonant letters <ck>.'

English orthography

An 'orthography' is the accepted way for spelling and writing words in a language. It is the conventional spelling system of that language: a system for making words permanent. Each written language has its own orthography. There are many different ones, but the thing they all share in common is that they use stylised graphic symbols in linear formations. English is an alphabetic orthography where the phonemes of the words are represented by letters. Writing goes along horizontal lines from left to right with the letters being produced in a left to right sequence. This contrasts with Chinese and Japanese writing, which is produced traditionally along vertical lines from top to bottom and then going from right to left across the page (though with the advent of computers this is changing). These orthographies use characters to represent whole concepts, they cannot be segmented down into the smaller phonological units of alphabetic writing.

What does it mean to say a language is alphabetic? The solution to the question of how to represent spoken language visually has been solved in alphabetic languages through the invention of 'alphabets'. These orthographies make use of a relatively small set of stylised graphic symbols (letters) which map onto small phonological units: phonemes (sounds) for representing every word. At its simplest children must learn the letter that relates to each specific phoneme and use this code to spell words, e.g. modern Turkish.[9] Unfortunately, for learning to spell in English, the orthography is not simple.

The 26-letter alphabet used in English is the Latin script. It is made up of 26 unique configurations of lines and curves. Though each letter is unique, some are mirror images (or near mirror images) of each other: e.g. b d, p q, s z; and some invert across the horizontal: e.g. h y, f t, n u, m w in some print fonts. When forming the letters by handwriting the motor pattern for each letter is unique. Learning to form the letters fluently is an important skill for spelling because if writers do not know how to form the individual letters their writing is indecipherable. When skilled handwriting is achieved, attention shifts from the physical production of the words to the content and structure of the text.[7,8] When writing via a keyboard, the position of the letter must be accessed for a press action to be executed. In this case, unlike handwriting, the form of the letter is not the result of a unique configuration of motor movements. Nevertheless, 'automatic' recognition of the letter shapes is necessary. Thus, whichever medium is used for text production, accurate letter knowledge is needed.

Each word has an 'orthographic identity', which is the sequence of letters that make up its visual form. Skilled readers and writers have this linked to its phonological (the sound), semantic (the meaning), and syntactic (the grammatical status) identities.[10] When this unique orthographic identity is stored there is word-specific knowledge of that word, which can be accessed directly when writing. The linkage of all four identities is important because in English there are some words that share their phonological identity but not their orthographic semantic or syntactic identities. These words are called 'homophonic-heterographs' (they sound the same but look different), e.g. *blew* and *blue*. Linking the orthographic identity of the individual words to their semantic and phonological identities enables correct spelling. Orthographic identities include order information. The left-right sequence for producing the letters is important. For example, *'art rat tar'* are all composed of the same letters so they could be said to look alike, but the different sequences are different words.

Sounds and spelling

Spoken language is composed of vowel phonemes and consonant phonemes, with more consonants than vowels. Spoken English has 44 phonemes, with the number varying slightly depending on the individual regional accents (both within and between countries). There is considerable variation of accent in spoken English within countries where English is the dominant language. However, there is no variation in spelling within countries, though there is between countries, e.g. *'colour'* in British English but *'color'* in American English. Accent is not represented in spelling, only generalised phonology. For example, the word meaning 'the thing one gets into to wash oneself' is <bath> but this is pronounced as /b æ θ/ (short vowel) or /b ɑ: θ/ (long vowel) depending on accent.

The 26 letters of the alphabet are used to represent the 44 phonemes. There are 24 are consonant phonemes and 20 are vowel phonemes, but the alphabet is composed of 21 consonant letters: <b c d f g h j k l m n p q r s t v w x y z> and only five vowel letters: <a e i o u>. <y> can sometimes represent a vowel phoneme /ai/ as in *fly*, and sometimes a consonant phoneme /j/ as in *yellow*. The lack of enough vowel letters for English phonemes is the result of an historical 'borrowing' of the Latin alphabet to represent the languages of the British Isles over the centuries. Latin had far fewer vowel phonemes so the Romans only needed the small set of vowel letters. Over the centuries the solutions to representing all the English vowel phonemes have been many and various, not consistent or transparent, which makes spelling vowel phonemes in English the most challenging aspect of word spelling.

Vowel phoneme spelling

In modern English there are six distinct short vowel phonemes, which are usually written with their canonical vowel letters: /æ/ *cat*; /ɛ/ *wet*; /i/ *sit*; / ɒ/ *plot*; /ʌ/ *duck*; and /ʊ/ which is also written using <u> *put*. There is a further indistinct short vowel phoneme called the *schwa* / ə /. This unstressed vowel phoneme is one of the most frequently occurring in continuous speech, but which has no consistent letter to represent it. For example, at the end of *ever* you can hear the sound /ə /, as in /ɛ v ə / spelt <er>. You hear the same sound at the end of *error*, as in /ɛ r ə / spelt <or>. Also, the indefinite article *a* is spelt <a>, but generally pronounced as a schwa, particularly in continuous speech.

Given the six distinct short vowels plus the schwa, this leaves a further 13 longer vowel phonemes which all require representation. In this instance, longer literally means that the sound lasts longer in time: the sound /ae / in *mad* is shorter that the sound /ei / in *maid*. In order to represent these vowels, the orthographic device of using more than one letter has been developed. Where letters are used to stand for one sound they must be parsed together and are called a *grapheme* or *digraph*: e.g. <ai> <ea> <oa> <ue> <oo> <al> <er> <ow> <oy>. Some vowel phonemes are represented by three or even four letters graphemes: <air> <eau> <igh> <eigh> <ough>. These examples show that vowel graphemes may be composed of two vowel letters or a vowel letter(s) plus a consonant letter(s). When consonant letters are part of a vowel grapheme they are not sounded. In graphemes composed of two vowel letters, the phoneme represented is usually the longer vowel phoneme of the first letter in the pair. Children are sometimes taught the spelling rule 'when two vowels go out walking, the first vowel does the talking': e.g. *rain, goal*. This can be helpful, but invariably there are exceptions to the rule: e.g. *great, feud, friend*.

The use of the term 'rule' in relation to English spelling should be treated with caution. It is more helpful to think of these as patterns that re-occur because there are always exceptions to the 'rules'.[11, 12]

In addition to the graphemes where the letters are parsed together to represent the vowel phonemes, there is a further orthographic pattern for representing long vowel phonemes. This is the *split vowel digraph*, or *marker E*. In the past children may have been taught about the 'magic E that makes the vowel say its name', i.e. the vowel represented is long. The orthographic pattern of a split vowel digraph is vowel letter followed by consonant letter, followed by <e> (<-VCE>), e.g. *bide, plane*. This pattern is almost a rule. Unsurprisingly there are exceptions. *Give* and *have* are high frequency words that look as though they obey the rule, but the vowel phoneme is short. The reason for this exception is that there is an orthographic 'rule' that overrides the phonological rule: namely English words do not end with <v>. This rule does not hold for neologisms like *spiv* (a word for a petty criminal coined during the Second World War), abbreviations like *improv,* or many names: *Shiv, Rav*. False split vowel digraphs also occur at the end of some polysyllabic words, e.g. *peregrine, glycerine, crinoline*. These pose challenges for learning to spell. When children are first taught the split vowel digraph rule they may begin to make errors by writing *hav* instead of *have* and *peregrin* instead of *peregrine*. This shows they have learnt the 'rule' then over applied it. Such errors can be considered positive, but particularly *hav* needs correcting so that an accurate orthographic identity is built up of this high frequency word. If *have* is continuously written as *hav*, the storage of the correct orthographic identity may be compromised leading to errors being produced when writing under stress.[13]

It might be supposed that the device of using digraphs could have solved the problem of representing the larger set of vowel phonemes in a systematic way. But, for many historic reasons, every vowel phoneme has at least two orthographic representations:

sit crystal	*wet head*	*cat plait*	*plot swan*	*duck some*
put could	*banana father*	*tree knead*	*girl learn*	*calf hard*
saw taught	*shoe crew*	*play eight*	*go sew*	*sigh my*
loud bough	*boy coin*	*fear deer*	*there their*	*pure your*

This list is not exhaustive, and you might like to play with identifying as many different graphemes of vowel phonemes as you can.[12]

Consonant phoneme spelling

The spelling of consonant phonemes is far less variable and inconsistent than vowel phonemes, but not without hazard. Some consonant phonemes are spelt with a single canonical consonant letter: /p/= <p>, /b/ = <b>, /t/ = <t>, /d/ = <d>, /g/ = goat /n/ = <n>, /l/ = <l>, /r/ = < r>, /j/ = < y>, /h/ = <h>. These mappings are the reverse of the letter-sound mappings that are learnt in phonics for reading. However, /p/ /b/ /t/ /d/ /g/ /n/ /l/ /r/ can also be spelt with a geminate – a doubled letter: *clipper rabble latter ladder giggle banner rolled barrel.* Doubling the consonant letter does not change the phoneme represented, but it may have an impact on the preceding vowel phoneme: e.g. *mate matte.*

There are five consonant phonemes that are always spelt with a digraph: /θ/ = <th> *thumb,* /ð/ = <th> they, /tʃ/ = <ch> *chocolate,* /ʃ/ = <sh> ship, and /ŋ/ = <ng>. Even here there is inconsistency because /ʃ/ can be <ch> as in chef or <ti> as in *station,* and /tʃ/ can be <-tch> at the ends of words.

A further characteristic of English orthography relates to positional constraints and the frequency of occurrence of patterns of word spellings. A feature of human learning is that we have a capacity to extract frequency information and statistical properties from the environment in which we are surrounded [14]. We learn about patterns and can use them in our behaviours. Through exposure to print we become sensitive to orthographic patterns and use them in writing. The spelling of the phoneme /tʃ/ illustrates this. The most frequent grapheme for /tʃ/ is <ch>: *chap, rich.* The alternative spelling <tch> represents exactly the same phoneme but is subject to positional constraints and never occurs at the beginning of words. When children are learning to spell they show a level of sensitivity to the positional frequency of graphemes and so rarely make errors by placing unpermitted graphemes at the beginnings of words.

Consonant phonemes written with consonant digraphs always have one of the letters silent. These patterns often relate to the etymology of the word and discussion of this can be highly motivating for developing children's vocabulary. Examples of silent letters are <b> in <mb> *lamb,* <g> in <gn> *gnaw,* <k> in <kn> *knight,* <w> in <wr> *write.* These patterns are different from the graphemes <th>, <ch> etc. because <mb> <gn> <kn> and <wr> represent phonemes which are usually written with their canonical letter: <m> <n> and <r>.

There are some consonant phonemes that are spelt with their canonical letter, but which also have alternative spellings. For example, the phoneme /s/ is spelt with <s> *sat,* <ss> *lass* or <c> *cent;* /k/ takes multiple forms: <k> *kit;* <c> *cat;* <ck> *back;* <ch> *choir;* and <que> *opaque.*

These examples of phoneme-grapheme pairings for vowels and consonants show how English spelling is inconsistent and complex. There is a lot to learn about the representation of the phonemes, about patterns, and about individual words. Nevertheless, every phoneme can be identified in a word's orthography. The one exception to this is words with <x> which represents two phonemes /ks/. In phonics programmes children are taught <x> = /ks/ as a blended consonant at the end of words or syllables, e.g. *six, expect.*

The phonemic basis of spelling means that it is important for children to become explicitly phonemically aware. They can then identify word structures by segmenting whole words into their component phonemes. Phonemic segmentation for spelling is harder than phoneme blending for reading.[15] If children are able to segment words into component phonemes, and have been taught phoneme-grapheme correspondences (PGCs), they are able to generate readable and plausible spellings of words. The issue is that PGC knowledge is essential but not sufficient because there are too many words that cannot be accurately spelled by application of these correspondences.

Morphemic aspects of spelling.

English is called a deep orthography because not only are the sounds represented, but so are aspects of morphology. Morphology is the system of language relating to how words are constructed relative to root meaning and affixes (prefixes and suffixes). Words are units of meaning: *morphemes*, with the morpheme being the smallest grammatical unit of language that has meaning. Prefixes and suffixes are also morphemes because they carry meaning, but not words in their own right. There are two types of affix: *inflectional* affixes and *derivational* affixes.

There are only a few inflectional affixes and they are always suffixes. These express grammatical contrasts but do not change the meaning of words. For example, the expression of the plural in English is via a plural inflexion added to the end of a noun. Phonologically this takes three forms: /s/ /z/ /ɪz/; *cat*+/s/, *dog*+/z/, *horse*+/ɪz/. However, in spelling orthography overrides phonology, so the plural affix is always spelt with the letter <s>: *cats, dogs, horses.* Children will almost certainly have internalised the phonology of the plural by the time they are becoming literate so they may represent phonology in misspellings such as *dogz* and *horsiz*. One can see why it is helpful to be taught the plural orthographic pattern to avoid errors.

Verb tenses are also expressed with inflectional suffixes. The past tense for regular weak verbs is formed phonologically by adding an affix: /d/ /t/ /ɪd/: *rain*+/d/, *kiss*+/t/, *want*+/ɪd/. Again in spelling orthography overrides phonology so the past tense marker is almost always spelt <ed> regardless of the phonology. However, you may be frowning at this point because the past tense of the verb to *spell* is here given as <spelt>. It is a delightful aspect of English that the word that relates to spelling itself has an irregular past tense marker of <t> in British English orthography. There are a few other examples of this irregularity: *learnt, burnt, dreamt*. Although the regular form *learned, burned* and *dreamed* is also permitted.

'Derivational' affixes can come at the beginning or the end of a word. There are a large number of derivational affixes, which may modify or change meaning and/or change word class. Here just a few are for exemplification. An example of a meaning changing affix is the prefix <un-> which reverses the meaning of the root: *undo*. <un-> is a prefix with consistent regular spelling, as are <pre->, <post->, <ante-> and <anti->.

Examples of derivational suffixes that change word class and have a regular spelling are <-ness>, <-ly>, <-less>. The morpheme <-ness> has the effect of changing an adjective into a noun: *glad → gladness*; <-ly> turns the adjective into an adverb *glad → gladly*; <-less> turns a verb into an adjective *help → helpless*, then with the further <-ness> the adjective becomes a noun *helplessness*.

Though there is a degree of consistency, not all affixes are regular in spelling. The morpheme, which is affixed to a verb of action to create an agent noun is pronounced /ə/ but it can be spelt <-er> or <-or> (and very infrequently <-ar> or <-ir>). Pupils could learn the specific orthography for every agent noun but there are some orthographic/phonological patterns to help; though there are always exceptions. Verbs ending in a single consonant, a consonant cluster, a consonant digraph or a split vowel digraph tend to take <-er>, e.g. *eater, builder, busker, maker*. Exceptions are *sailor, inventor, supervisor*. Verbs ending in <-ct> and polysyllabic verbs ending in <-ate> and <-it> tend to take <-or>, e.g. *actor, educator, editor*. Engaging with affixation supports spelling development and at the same time helps to develop vocabulary and morphological awareness.[16, 17, 18] Both of which support the development of text writing.

Another example where orthography and morphology interact is with the conditional rules called 'doubling and dropping'. When a suffix is attached to a word which takes the phonological form consonant(s)-short vowel-consonant – e.g *hop* – the final consonant letter is doubled to 'preserve' the short vowel – *hop, hopping, hopped*. When the vowel in a /CVC/ word is long and spelt with a split vowel digraph, the final <e> is dropped before the affix is added – *hope, hoping, hoped*. Application of the correct rule gives the following patterns: *hop, hopping, hopped and hope, hoping, hoped*. Application of the rule incorrectly leads to real words with but wrong meaning → *hop – hoping, hoped* and *hope, hoping, hopped.*

This short account of English orthography shows that it is not possible to learn to spell accurately entirely by the application of PGCs or entirely by learning 'rules' but all this knowledge can be helpful. Orthographic patterns and morphology are also useful. The complex nature of the orthography leads to people implicitly orchestrating different strategies to become fluent spellers.[11] Acknowledging this when teaching is effective.

How we spell words

One account of how we spell words proposes that there are two routes.[19, 20, 21, 22] and a more recent model proposes that people spell through the integration of multiple patterns.[14, 23, 24, 25, 26]

A dual route model of word spelling

Dual route models propose a direct route to word spelling called the 'addressed' route and a second route called the 'assembled route'. A word is said to be spelt by the addressed route when a stored representation with the letters in the correct sequence is accessed and the letters are then written down in serial order. This word-specific pattern is the word's orthographic identity. If this is correct, producing words by this route leads to accurate spelling. This suggests that it is important to establish accurate orthographic identities because incorrect identities lead to incorrect spelling. The greater the number of words stored in this way, the more accurate whole written texts are likely to be.

The question is: how do words get stored? This could be by rote-learning, but it is more likely that an assembled route is established, which leads to the creation of the orthographic identity. When a word is spelt by the assembled route, the target word is segmented into its component phonemes. These are then mapped onto a sequence of letters or graphemes which are then assembled. The same processes as for the addressed route are used to write down the sequence of letters. In English, spelling a word by this route may lead to phonologically plausible but not necessarily accurate spelling.

In the learning phase of becoming literate, the two routes to spelling need to be established. This is not a conscious process but one that is supported through effective teaching and opportunities for practice. Initially children will have very few stored orthographic identities of words, so they need to use PGCs to generate words. This means they need phoneme-grapheme knowledge. Through repeated application of PGCs, word-specific knowledge is established so words can then be spelt via the addressed route.

Integration of multiple patterns (IMP) framework

In their alternative to the dual route, Treiman and Kessler (2014)[26] base their IMP framework on the fact that writing systems include a range of features, and on the capacity of humans for statistical learning. By multiple exposures to words in many different textual contexts they are able to implicitly extract letter patterns, e.g. <ough> *rough, through, bought*, which reoccur in words but are not necessarily linked to a stable phonology. They also extract morphological patterns (affixations). This reduces the cognitive demands on establishing word-specific information. Addressed and assembled spellings are incorporated in the IMP framework.

Learning to spell

It was thought that spelling developed through a sequence of stages:[27, 28]

1. A *pre-communicative stage* when 'writing' would be a sequence of letters with spaces that looked like words but with no relation to phonology.

2. A *semi-phonetic stage* when children began to be aware of relationship between letters and sounds.

3. A *phonetic stage* where all the phonemes of the word would be represented with letters but only those words with regular grapheme-phoneme spelling would be likely to be accurate.

4. A *transitional stage* when children would begin to incorporate common letter patterns and so move away from a dependence on pure phonology and phoneme-grapheme mapping.

5. The *correct stage* when children were able to incorporate multiple sources of knowledge of orthography including morphology, phonology, orthographic patterns and word-specific knowledge. The data source for the demarcation of these stages was from examples of children's errors produced when writing spontaneously.

Though a stage-like development seemed plausible, further research cast doubt on the simplicity of this.[29, 30, 31] Children's writing showed use of multiple sources of knowledge to generate the spelling of words, but for which, as yet, they did not have word-specific knowledge. Thus, in the same piece of writing the errors <beged> for *begged*, <startid> for *started*, <cold> for *could*, and <woh> for *who* might be found, whilst at the same time spelling *wanted*, *over* and *their* correctly. These errors show awareness of the sound structure of the target word with evidence of knowledge of orthographic patterns and morphology. In their writing, right from the start, children use multiple sources of knowledge to generate spellings and this casts doubt on spelling development being stage-like. If children can use phonology, word-specific knowledge, morphology and awareness of orthographic patterns simultaneously then an account of spelling based on the integration of multiple patterns seems to account for more of the behaviour. This points the way to effective teaching providing children information about phonology, orthography and morphology.

Teaching spelling

Much of the early evidence about spelling development came from studying children's writing generated in situations where they were allowed to produce texts 'unhindered' by direct teaching.[32] However, just as it is now recognised that children find it easier to learn to read if they receive direct instruction, so there is evidence that children learn to spell more accurately if they are explicitly taught. But what should they be taught? The logical conclusion from insights about English orthography and the IMP framework point to children being taught multiple strategies.[25, 26]

Since English is an alphabetic orthography, learning phonics for spelling is one obvious strategy. Phonics for spelling means learning PGCs. Children, therefore, need explicit phoneme awareness and word segmentation skills in order to use their PGC knowledge. Segmentation for spelling is harder than blending for reading and requires a higher degree of accuracy so that each phoneme is identified. This requires supported practice.

Learning phonics provides a good entry into spelling, but it is not enough. Many of the high frequency content words needed to create grammatically accurate meaningful texts are not transparent, e.g. *so, was, be, where, their*. Children need word-specific orthographic identities established of these early on in their literacy education. Generating phonologically plausible but incorrect spellings without feedback on accuracy leads to formation of incorrect orthographic identities. Spelling when writing under pressure may become unstable. Teachers have to find a fine line between feedback ensuring accuracy without demotivating children.

Through exposure to print whilst reading children become sensitive to orthographic patterns. Reading supports spelling development. Through their teaching of text reading and vocabulary, teachers can support children's use of multiple strategies for generating word spellings. Having explicit attention drawn to patterns in multiple words helps to establish these, and this then can feed into the extension of word-specific knowledge.

At the beginning of this chapter, the point was made that spelling is at the service of text writing. It is very rare for a sentence to be composed of monomorphemic root words in English, therefore teaching children about affixation in spelling can support writing. Explicit teaching about orthographic patterns and spelling 'rules' relative to affixation is generative and supports spelling development more than simply requiring children to memorise the spelling of words.[16, 33] One teaching approach can be to provide children with sets of words that can be divided into subsets based orthographic features. Through being asked to derive patterns, children can develop insights about orthography and extend their vocabulary.

In the past teaching spelling tended to be based on an assumption that through writing out multiple lists of words children would become competent spellers. The lists might have been composed of words that shared common spelling patterns or words in semantic relationships. The occasional 'rule' would also feature, but the teaching was not strategic. If teachers know about the nature of English orthography and about the strategies adult competent spellers use, then they understand what to teach. They will understand that children need to be taught how to spell words through the operation of multiple strategies. Exposure to print helps to build up orthographic knowledge and vocabulary, but children need multiple opportunities to create texts. They need to spell words in meaningful contexts to build up their ability to spell 'automatically'. Vocabulary continues to grow throughout life so utilisation of phonology, orthography and morphology will always be needed for words that have not yet gained a stored orthographic identity.

References

1. Berninger, V., Vaughan, K., Abbott, R., Begay, K., Coleman, K., Curtin, G., Hawkins, J. and Graham, S. (2002) 'Teaching spelling and composition alone and together: Implications for the simple view of writing', *Journal of Educational Psychology* 94 pp. 291-304.

2. Gough, P. B. and Tunmer, W. E. (1986) 'Decoding, reading, and reading disability', *Remedial and Special Education* 7 (1) pp. 6-10.

3. Berninger, V. and Amtmann, D. (2003) 'Preventing written expression disabilities through early and continuing assessment and intervention for handwriting and/or spelling problems: Research into practice' in Swanson, H., Harris, K. and Graham, S. (eds) *Handbook of Learning Disabilities.* New York, NY: The Guilford Press, pp. 323-344.

4. Berninger, V. and Winn, W. (2006) 'Implications of advancements in brain research and technology for writing development, writing instruction, and educational evolution' in MacArthur, C., Graham, S. and Fitzgerald, J. (eds) *Handbook of Writing Research.* New York, NY: The Guilford Press, pp. 96-114.

5. Kellogg, R. T. (1996) 'A model of working memory in writing' in Levy, C. M. and Ransdell, S. (eds) *The science of writing: Theories, methods, individual differences, and applications.* Mahwah, NJ: Lawrence Erlbaum Associates, p. 5771.

6. Olive T. (2004) 'Working memory in writing: Empirical evidence from the dual-task technique', *European Psychologist* 9 (1) pp. 32-42.

7. Connelly, V., Dockrell, J. and Barnett, J. (2005) 'The slow handwriting of undergraduate students constrains overall performance in exam essays', *Educational Psychology* 25 (1) pp. 99-107.

8. Stainthorp, R. and Rauf, N. (2009) 'An investigation of the influence of the transcription skills of handwriting and spelling on the quality of text writing by girls and boys in Key Stage 2', *Handwriting Today* 8 (1) pp. 8-14.

9. Babayiğit, S. and Stainthorp, R. W. (2010) 'Component processes of early reading, spelling, and narrative writing skills in Turkish: a longitudinal study', *Reading and Writing: An Interdisciplinary Journal* 23 (5) pp. 539-568.

10. Ehri, L. C. (1980) 'The development of orthographic images' in Frith, U. (ed) *Cognitive processes in spelling*. London: Academic Press, pp. 311-338.

11. Carney, E. (1994) *A survey of English spelling*. Abingdon: Routledge.

12. Carney, E. (2014) *English Spelling*. Abingdon: Routledge.

13. Wing, A. M. and Baddeley, A. (1980) 'Spelling errors in handwriting: a corpus and a distributional analysis' in Frith, U. (ed) *Cognitive Processes in Spelling*. London: Academic Press, pp. 251-285.

14. Treiman, R. (2018) 'Statistical learning and spelling', *Language, Speech, and Hearing Sciences in Schools* 49 (1) pp. 644-652.

15. Stainthorp, R. and Hughes, D. (2004) 'What happens to precocious readers' performance by the age of eleven?' *Journal of Research in Reading* 27 (4) pp. 357-372.

16. Nunes, T. and Bryant, B. (2009) *Children's reading and spelling: Beyond The first steps*. Chichester: Wiley-Blackwell.

17. Nunes, T., Bryant, P. and Bindman, M. (1997) 'Morphological spelling strategies: Developmental stages and processes', *Developmental Psychology* 33 (4) pp. 637-49.

18. Nunes, T., Bryant, P. and Olsson, J. (2003) 'Learning Morphological and Phonological Spelling Rules: An Intervention Study', *Scientific Studies of Reading* 7 (3) pp. 289-307.

19. Brown, G. D. A. and Loosemore, R. P. W. (1994) 'Computational approaches to normal and impaired spelling' in Brown, G. D. A. and Ellis, N. C. (eds) *Handbook of spelling: Theory, process and application*. Chichester: John Wiley & Sons.

20. Campbell, R. (1987) 'One or two lexicons for reading and writing words: Can misspellings shed any light?' *Cognitive Neuropsychology* 4 (4) pp. 487-499.

21. Caramazza, A. (1988) 'Some aspects of language processing revealed through the analysis of acquired dysgraphia: The lexical system', *Annals of Neuroscience* 11 pp. 395-421.

22. Tainturier, M. J. and Rapp, B. (2000) 'The spelling process' in Rapp, B. (ed) *The Handbook of Cognitive Neuropsychology*. Ann Arbor, MI: Edwards, pp. 263-280.

23. Apel, K., Wilson-Fowler, E. B., Brimo, D. and Perrin N. A. (2012) 'Metalinguistic contributions to reading and spelling in second and third grade students', *Reading and Writing: An Interdisciplinary Journal* 25 (6) pp. 1283-1305.

24. Treiman, R. (2017) 'Learning to spell: Phonology and beyond', *Cognitive Neuropsychology* 34 (3-4) pp. 83-93.

25. Treiman, R. (2017) 'Learning to spell words: Findings, theories, and issues', *Scientific Studies of Reading* 21 pp. 265-276.

26. Treimen, R. and Kessler, B. (2014) *How children learn to write words.* Oxford: Oxford University Press.

27. Gentry, R. J. (1982) 'An Analysis of Developmental Spelling in 'GNYS AT WRK', *The Reading Teacher* 36 (2) pp. 192-200.

28. Henderson, E. H. and Beers, J. W. (1980) *Developmental and cognitive aspects of learning to spell: a reflection of word knowledge.* Newark, DE: International Reading Association.

29. Kwong, T. E. and Varnhagen, C. K. (2005) 'Strategy Development and Learning to Spell New Words: Generalization of a Process', *Developmental Psychology* 41 (1) pp. 148-159

30. Rittle-Johnson, B. and Siegler, R. S. (1999) 'Learning to spell: Variability, choice, and change in children's strategy use', *Child Development* 70 (2) pp. 332-348.

31. Varnhagen, C. K., McCallum, M. and Burstow, M. (1997) 'Is children's spelling naturally stage-like?' *Reading and Writing: An Interdisciplinary Journal* 9 (5-6) pp. 451-481.

32. Treiman, R. (1993) *Beginning to spell: a study of first-grade children.* New York, NY: Oxford University Press.

33. Nicholson, T. and Dymock, S. (2017) 'To what extent does children's spelling improve as a result of learning words with the look, say, cover, write, check, fix strategy compared with phonological spelling strategies?' *Australian Journal of Learning Difficulties* 22 (2) pp. 1-17.

WRITING SKILLS

BY TOM NEEDHAM

Are good writers born or made? Certainly, some people have an affinity for writing, in the same way that some of us have an affinity for languages. The field of writing is enormous, and professional writers can spend a lifetime honing their craft. But for all of us, the ability to express ourselves clearly, concisely and in a form appropriate to the purpose are essential. In this chapter, Tom Needham draws on some of the research around explicit instruction in writing to contend that specific, systematic practice, built on carefully developed skill sequences, can result in students who are more confident, articulate writers. In the time-limited world of classroom teaching, he focuses on high-leverage strategies that enable students to develop essential competencies quickly. This chapter is essential reading if you work with students who struggle with sentence structure.

Author bio-sketch:

Tom Needham is Research Lead and Head of English at Trinity School. Before his current role, he taught in International Schools in Penang, Malaysia and Lagos, Nigeria. He has also previously taught EFL in Thailand and Harrogate as well as history, citizenship, sociology, geography, media studies and RE in Croydon. His teaching interests include Engelmann's DI, grammar, Cognitive Load Theory, memory, and knowledge-rich curricula. He blogs at www.tomneedhamteach. wordpress.com

Teaching writing

In the book *Practice Perfect*, the writers posit that 'the skills you see in your top performers are the very skills you then work to develop in everyone on your team' and that a 'disciplined approach to identifying top performers and analysing top performance provides you with the curriculum'.[1] If these ideas are applied to the field of writing instruction, then we are forced to ask the question: what are the elements of good writing? 'Good writing' is an amorphous and nebulous term. Clearly, there is not one definitive style, approach or list of constituent elements that results in good writing and if there was, that would only serve to remove the wonder, the beauty and the personal, potentially resulting in the sterile and the functional, creating a tick-box approach that is both bland and formulaic. However, the fact that the ingredients of good writing are varied and wide-ranging should not preclude attempting to teach some of them.

Explicitly teaching specific sentence styles and grammatical constructions to students can help them to broaden their range of expression, moving them from functional and simplistic written communication to sophisticated, nuanced and complex writing. Although excellence comes in myriad forms and styles, there are some sentence styles that we would closely and, perhaps, even exclusively associate with sophisticated writing and, while many examples of excellence may avoid these constructions, the ability to use these styles would go some way towards improving the technicality and proficiency of a student's written output.

Teaching phrases at Key Stage 3 (participles, appositives and absolutes) is one high utility strategy because these constructions can be used across the broad genres of writing that are required in GCSE language and literature (textual analysis, rhetoric and description):

Noun appositive examples:

1. **Textual analysis:** Utterson, *an 'austere' man who avoids pleasure and frivolity in order to maintain his reputation*, is obsessed with propriety and decorum.

2. **Description:** The man clutched his satchel, *a tattered bag which contained his meagre possessions.*

3. **Rhetoric:** *A shame, a tragedy, an embarrassment*, their defeat sent shockwaves across the sporting community.

If we teach the component parts of a sentence, then they can be combined, manipulated and generalised by students into an immense number of combinations. While morphographs are the building blocks of words, phrases are some of the building blocks of sentences and can be combined in lots of different ways when writing. Here are a few examples of how these sub components can be combined:

Combinations	
Double absolute	*His words verging on the prophetic, his 'fire blood and anguish' rhetoric lifted straight from the bible,* the inspector's final speech is a dire warning about the consequences of an atomised society.
Double noun appositive	*A 'hard headed man of business',* Mr Birling is convinced that sacking Eva Smith, *an action that began the chain of events that led to her death,* was the correct thing to do.
Double present participle	*Speaking in a commanding tone, interjecting 'massively',* the inspector exudes authority and expertly deals with 'one line of enquiry at a time.'
Present participle at the start. Noun apposite at the end	*Subscribing to a hierarchical model of society,* Mrs Birling clearly enjoys the power that she gets not only from her wealth, but also from being chairwoman of a charity, *a position that she uses to assert her authority rather than as a means of genuinely helping the poor.*

Once students have mastered the concept of a sentence and can parse sentences fairly well, naming nouns, verbs and other word classes, students can be taught how to use phrases, specifically participle, appositive and absolute phrases, building on Key Stage 2 and attempting to follow Engelmann's comment that 'for mastery teaching to be possible, programs must be thoroughly coordinated from level to level'.[2] One of his criticisms of traditional programs is that 'different levels of traditional programs present the same topics and the same examples.'[3] We don't want to merely repeat the grammar that they are taught in Key Stage 2 – we want to take them a step further. In Key Stage 3 English, we should teach the aspects of sentence construction that go beyond functional, everyday communication and usage – the kind of sentences that people rarely use in everyday oral communication, even in formalised, academic speech, yet are regularly found in high quality writing.

Many of our students do not read widely and, in the absence of fully guided instruction[4] and deliberate, focused practice, would be extremely unlikely to be able to use and manipulate these constructions. Those that do read widely may have developed a partial understanding or at least a vague familiarity with them. When teaching these constructions for the first time – particularly appositive and absolute phrases – it is common to hear assertions that the examples don't make sense, or that they are grammatically incorrect, evidence of just how unfamiliar some students are with these type of sentences. Thankfully, this initial confusion soon disappears and, given the right amount of explicit instruction and practice, students are quickly able to produce their own examples, dramatically broadening the range of sentences that they can use and increasing the sophistication and complexity of their writing.

Although I want my students to be able to name these particular parts of a sentence, most importantly I want them to use and apply them in their own writing. While there may be disagreement about the 'correct' name to give these (absolute phrases seem to be known as 'nominative absolutes' as well as 'noun phrases… combined with participles'), we still need a name to give them if we are to discuss, analyse and practice them, creating what Lemov refers to as 'a shared language for your team'.[5] If we have this shared language, we are able to minimise confusion and be precise, allowing us to create focused practice activities. Asking a student to write four noun appositive sentences about Bayonet Charge allows precise feedback to be given, as the success criteria are explicit and clear. In such an activity, both teacher and student understand the precise styles of sentence that is being asked for.

Choosing high utility sentence constructions is important and if students are to master them, they will need extended, distributed and varied practice, ideally spread across texts and units.

Track system planning

We often underestimate the amount of distributed practice a student will require before they are able to retain and master what is being taught. Quickly moving through content with no thought as to the necessity of recap and extended practice will almost always result in a lack of mastery and proficiency from students. Novices require extensive and distributed practice on new material if they are to truly master it. Initial teaching should span two or three consecutive lessons[6] and then practice exercises that ask students to apply what has been taught should be distributed across many more.

The idea of a 'spiral curriculum' is common across subjects: in English it might mean 'doing' poetry once a year for five years in the hope that if they don't get it the first time, there will be further opportunities to do so. While the spiral approach to curriculum planning is commonplace across subjects, Engelmann points out a number of flaws. Firstly, it creates a low expectation for performance as students are merely 'exposed' to content without any real expectation for mastery. Secondly, students quickly come to realise that the information and concepts that are being taught are temporary and will soon be replaced with another unit that 'does not require application of skills and knowledge from the previous unit'. It is almost as if the spiral curriculum, by its very design and approach, reinforces apathy and a lack of application. If you knew that you would not need to use or be asked to use a concept again, then it might be entirely rational to give it less than the desired level of effort and thought. Disposable content fosters indifference.

The alternative to a spiral curriculum, and the approach favoured by Engelmann's DI schemes, is called the strand curriculum.[7]

Illustration of spiral versus strand curriculum
adapted from Snider and Crawford (2004)

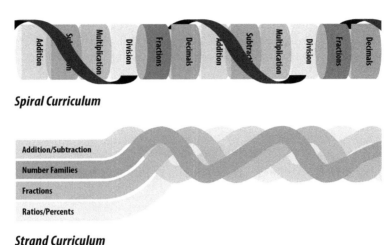

Figure 1. Illustration of spiral versus strand curriculum[8]

Strand Curricula weave multiple objectives through lessons, each incrementally increasing in complexity as students become more proficient at what is being taught. I teach some of Engelmann's Direct Instruction programmes and one of the key theoretical ideas behind the Strand Curriculum is that concepts are taught to and used by students across a number of lessons and weeks, the intention being not just retention but also fluency and mastery of the material. A gradual progression from restricted, closed practice activities – for example, sentence drills – to wider application in extended writing is also common across DI programmes, one of the aims being to slowly and methodically convert 'inflexible' into more 'flexible' knowledge.[9]

Following Engelmann's guidance, an instructional sequence for writing should be methodically planned out so that each step forward is both manageable and small enough[10] for all students to experience a high success rate. Instruction should broadly follow an I-we-you format,[11] gradually fading out support in order to account for the incremental development of expertise. If learners are deemed to be novices, then at the beginning of the instructional sequence

– the 'I' stage-worked examples should be used in order to provide 'schema substitutes', helping them overcome the limitation of their working memory and slowly building their background knowledge.[12] An optimal approach is known as 'the alternation strategy' where students study a worked example and then immediately complete a similar application.[13] Towards the end of an instructional sequence, the 'you' stage learners should increasingly be asked to apply what has been taught in extended writing. By retrieving and applying their developing background knowledge, learners can begin to develop automaticity as well as increasing the storage and retrieval strength of their schemas.

When teaching writing explicitly – both at sentence and paragraph level – the use of worked examples and backwards fading can help students achieve a consistently high success rate, as well as ensuring that learning is as efficient as possible.

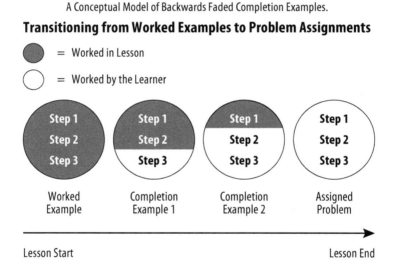

A Conceptual Model of Backwards Faded Completion Examples.

Transitioning from Worked Examples to Problem Assignments

= Worked in Lesson

= Worked by the Learner

Step 1	Step 1	Step 1	Step 1
Step 2	Step 2	Step 2	Step 2
Step 3	Step 3	Step 3	Step 3
Worked Example	Completion Example 1	Completion Example 2	Assigned Problem

Lesson Start   Lesson End

Figure 2. A conceptual model of backwards fading[14]

The instructional sequence that follows demonstrates the application of backwards fading and the gradual progression from worked examples to completion examples and then finally to assigned problems. The sequence focuses entirely on subject matter that is being taught – in this case GCSE literature texts – therefore developing writing skills as well as deepening understanding of content.[15]

Lesson 1

Step one: Present and label examples

1. *A poem that denounces exploitation,* London conveys the omnipresence of suffering.

2. Ozymandias, *a poem that highlights the transience of human power,* demonstrates that nobody is immortal.

3. *A callous capitalist who disdains collective responsibility,* Mr.Birling is only concerned with 'lower costs and higher prices'.

Depending on the class, this may be entirely teacher led or may involve a series of questions asking students to help with labelling: What is the subject of the sentence? Where is the verb? What is London? It is a poem that denounces exploitation. What is Ozymandias? It is a poem that demonstrates the transience of human power.

Adding arrows, prompts and labels to example sentences[16] can help make the implicit interactions and relationships between different components obvious to students, helping to focus attention on what is being taught.

Step two: Begin further examples and ask students to orally complete them

Teacher writes a half-completed example under the visualiser:

1. A manipulative woman who berates her husband, Lady Macbeth

With a weaker class, the teacher may want to give several completed oral examples before asking students to attempt their own. Students can then complete the sentence orally, a task that allows students to experience success before even attempting to write their own answers. Stronger students can offer ideas first, allowing weaker students to hear further examples before attempting it themselves. Asking students to narrate the punctuation in their spoken sentence (*A manipulative woman who berates her husband* **comma** *Lady Macbeth...*) not only helps to draw students' attention to the necessity of punctuation in the construction but it also 'overtises' the process, making it easy for a teacher to observe and give precise feedback to the student.[17] In the initial stages of instruction, corrective feedback should be immediate, preventing errors from becoming ingrained.

To further focus the practice or raise the level of challenge, the teacher could ask students to include specific things in their completed oral sentences by writing prompts.[18] This is deliberate practice: by practicing narrow and specific tasks, students can improve more efficiently.[19]

Example:

1. A manipulative woman who berates her husband, Lady Macbeth

Include:

- *'pour my spirits in my ear'*
- sinister

Step three: Begin further examples and ask students to complete them in writing

Students are presented with a series of half completed examples and are asked to complete them. With weaker classes, it may be useful to complete an example or two under the visualiser, narrating your thought process so that students know exactly what they are supposed to do.

1. A tyrannical and vainglorious King, Ozymandias

2. Hyde, a sadistic character who _____, **seems**

3. A criticism of _____, **An Inspector calls encourages the audience to**

4. The archetypal Victorian gentleman, Utterson

Because of the restricted nature of these completion problems, precise and immediate feedback can be given by the teacher. Students can be asked to read out their sentence, again narrating the punctuation so that the teacher – or students for that matter – can ascertain whether it is correct or not. This is a much faster feedback loop than taking all the books in and marking them. The teacher can then ask further questions to the student who gave the sentence (or different students) about the completed construction in order to draw attention to the function of the appositive or to provide further retrieval practice about the content of the sentence.

Example:

Student: *The archetypal Victorian gentleman* **comma** *Utterson is 'austere' and secretive* **comma** *avoiding fun at all costs.*

Possible teacher questions: Read out just the appositive. Who does it rename? What does archetypal mean? Which word in the sentence is a quotation? What does 'austere' mean? What specific things does Utterson do that make him 'austere'? Is he always like this? Why is his secrecy a form of duality?

The questions ask students about the grammatical structure as well as the content that is being taught, developing writing skills, as well as subject knowledge.[20]

As with the oral completion exercises, the level of challenge can be raised by asking students to include specific things in their answers, helping them to make links and connections between different bits of knowledge.

Example:

2. The archetypal Victorian gentleman, Utterson

Include:

- **'repressed'**
- *'never lighted with a smile'*
- contrived socialising with Enfield

In Expressive Writing 2, a Direct Instruction writing scheme, most lessons end with a single or multi-paragraph piece of writing and students are asked to complete a series of precise checks when they have completed their writing in order to ensure that they have applied a necessary skill and avoided making common, careless errors. This approach is also useful to the everyday classroom: instead of asking students to check their work – a vague statement that may be interpreted by students as 'skim read a bit of it' – it can be useful to specify exactly what they are checking for. These common errors can either be based upon what is being taught (the most likely mistakes that students will make when attempting the task) or they can be based upon the class that you teach, having been chosen as a result of feedback to the teacher. If a weaker class is on average bad at using full stops, then include that as a check. As in Expressive Writing, I would ask students to complete one check at a time in order to prevent cognitive overload.

Possible example checks for noun appositives:

Check 1: Does your appositive rename a noun that is right beside it?

Check 2: Is your appositive separated from the rest of the sentence with a comma or pair of commas?

Check 3: Does your sentence end with a full stop? (This check would be unnecessary for more proficient students!)

You may have noticed that I have still not asked students to complete problems on their own and this is deliberate. I want students to experience quick, initial success with writing these structures and spending time and effort on worked examples and completion problems allows this to happen. By doing so, even weaker students can experience high initial levels of success, something that both Engelmann and Rosenshine have identified is of crucial importance in instructional sequences.[21] If students are successful, this raises their motivation levels:[22] even the most apathetic students can become enthused if it is clear that they can succeed.

One lesson is not enough, however. Initial instruction should take place over a minimum of two lessons[23] and instruction and practice should continue in a track system across multiple lessons so that students develop fluency and automaticity. During the acquisition stage of learning, it may be helpful to have multiple practice opportunities in order for students to become proficient with a concept. As the sequence progresses, this practice should become increasingly more distributed in order to aid retention.[24]

The instructional sequence should aim to broadly follow the idea of backwards fading, slowly removing prompts and scaffolding so that students eventually apply their knowledge independently and without support. Finally, tasks should slowly change from isolated and decontextualised sentence practice to wider application within paragraphs and extended writing.

Here is a rough overview of what might happen in subsequent lessons:

Lessons 2, 3, 4, 5 and 6: Further worked examples and completion problems

Although the first lesson that I described would probably be a dedicated 'appositives' lesson, the subsequent lessons would more likely be practice tasks within lessons that contain many other foci.

While earlier lessons saw the teacher leading the labelling and annotation of the worked examples, as students become more proficient, they can be asked to do this themselves. The completion problems would be less restrictive, giving the students more autonomy and requiring them to complete more of the steps themselves. While the earlier completion problems provided the noun that does the renaming (a vainglorious and tyrannical king, Ozymandias…) the examples below require students to generate it for themselves:

Examples:

1. Hyde, a _____, is the opposite to
2. A _____, Lady Macbeth
3. A _____, The Prelude

Lesson 7, 8 and 9: Interleaved completion problems

These lessons may ask students to complete a range of different sentence styles, interleaving appositive practice with other constructions. In the example below, semicolon practice is mixed up with appositive practice. As with the appositives, students would have already completed the 'I and We' stages with semicolons before encountering them in this interleaved exercise.

Example:

1. A denunciation of _____, London _____
2. The Inspector admonishes the Birlings for their callousness; he wants
3. Macbeth's sword 'smoked with bloody execution', an image that demonstrates _____
4. Lady Macbeth, a manipulative _____, berates _____
5. Duncan is oblivious to their plans; he _____.

Lesson 10, 11 and 12: Independent problems

At some point, the worked examples become unnecessary and redundant, as students will have developed a mental conception of what it is that is being taught.[25] Instead of studying a model, they can retrieve the relevant schema from their long-term memory when attempting the task. Asking students to write a few specific sentences as a starter is a useful exercise.

Later lessons: Wider application

Once students have demonstrated the ability to accurately produce the construction in isolated drills, they can be asked to write a paragraph that contains noun appositives as one of the success criteria. Later still, they should apply the constructions to more extended essay type answers.

General principles

1. How long should you spend on each stage of the backwards fading continuum?

If we are to maximise efficiency in our instructional sequences – a key and important goal given that lesson time is finite – then we need to carefully consider two competing demands. Firstly, we should ensure that students have a high success rate: at least 70-80% for new material[26] and even higher for material that is being practiced and firmed.[27] Using worked examples and completion problems can make this level of success a reality, helping to minimise unwanted cognitive load. Secondly, we should use backwards fading so that students are asked to complete applications independently as quickly as possible. If we keep presenting worked examples, then not only will this waste time, but it may also prevent students from developing the ability to complete tasks without support. The example lessons above are an attempt to show how support should be faded, following the I-we-you continuum and ending with independent student application. How long students spend on each stage of the continuum is an empirical question and will largely be determined by the quality of examples and completion problems that you use as well as the proficiency and prior knowledge of the students. Feedback to the teacher is key here: if students are performing successfully on a stage, then you can make the transition to a lower level of support, increasing the number of steps that a student is expected to complete.

2. How do you optimise practice drills?

Practice sentences should probably involve content from whatever it is students are studying, as this will stretch and develop their thinking about the subject matter[28]. Not only will students be developing their writing skills, but they will also be deepening their understanding of the content.

In *Teach Like a Champion*, Lemov explains 'At Bats', the idea that 'succeeding once or twice at a skill won't bring mastery, give your students lots and lots of practice mastering knowledge or skills'. This is crucial. When students are asked to complete problems independently, they should practice extensively, ideally across a number of lessons and including 'multiple formats and with a significant number of plausible variations'. Here are some of the possible variations when teaching appositives:

- Varying where the appositive is in a sentence (start, embedded or the end)
- Varying the writing genre for the task (analytical, descriptive, rhetorical)
- Varying the content (*Macbeth, An Inspector Calls*)
- Adding quotations to the appositive
- Varying the number of appositives in a sentence
- Varying the length and level of detail within the appositive: adding 'who/that' is a great way of adding further description
- When they have mastered all of the above, integrating the appositive with other sentence styles that you are teaching

In summary, when teaching component skills for writing:

- Student success rate should be consistently high.
- Instructional sequences should move from worked examples to completion problems to independent practice, gradually fading out teacher support.
- Practice exercises should move from being restricted drills to wider application.
- Initial examples should involve prompts, labels and additional information to focus student attention.
- During the initial stages of an instructional sequence, practice should be massed; as the sequence progresses, this practice should become increasingly more distributed.
- At the beginning of an instructional sequence, feedback should be immediate and precise, preventing errors from becoming embedded.

References

1. Lemov, D., Woolway, E. and Yezzi, K. (2012) *Practice Perfect: 42 Rules for Getting Better at Getting Better.* San Francisco, CA: Jossey-Bass.

2. Engelmann, S. (2014) *Successful and Confident Students with Direct Instruction.* Eugene, OR: NIFDI Press.

3. Ibid.

4. Kirschner, P., Sweller, J. and Clark, R. (2006) 'Why Minimal Guidance During Instruction Does Not Work: An Analysis of the Failure of Constructivist, Discovery, Problem-Based, Experiential, and Inquiry-Based', *Teaching* Educational Psychologist 41 (2) pp. 75-86.

5. Ibid (n 1)

6. Ibid (n 2)

7. Snider, V. (2004) 'A Comparison of Spiral vs Strand Curriculum', *Journal of Direct Instruction* 4 (1) pp. 29-39.

8. Snider, V. E. and Crawford, D. (2004) 'Mathematics' in Marchand-Martella, N. E., Slocum, T. A. and Martella, R. C. (eds) *Introduction to Direct Instruction.* Boston: Allyn & Bacon, pp. 206-245.

9. Willingham, D. (2002) 'Ask the Cognitive Scientist. Inflexible Knowledge: The First Step to Expertise', *American Educator* 26 (4) pp. 31-33.

10. Ibid (n 2)

11. Lemov, D. (2010) *Teach Like a Champion: 49 Techniques That Put Students On The Path To College.* San Francisco, CA: Jossey-Bass.

12. Sweller, J., Ayres, P. and Kalyuga, S. (2011) *Cognitive Load Theory: Explorations in the Learning Sciences Instructional Systems and Performance Technologies.* New York, NY: Springer.

13. Clark, R., Nguyen, F. and Sweller, J. (2006) *Efficiency in Learning: Evidence Based Guidelines to Manage Cognitive Load*. San Francisco, CA: John Wiley and Sons.

14. Ibid.

15. Hochman, J.and Wexler, N. (2017) *The Writing Revolution*. San Francisco, CA: Jossey-Bass.

16. Watkins, C. and Slocum, T. (2004) 'The Components of Direct Instruction', *Journal of Direct Instruction* 3 (2) pp. 7-11.

17. Engelmann, S. and Carnine, D. (2016) *Theory of Instruction*. Eugene, OR: NIFDI Press.

18. Ibid (n 16)

19. Christodolou, D., (2017) *Making Good Progress? The Future of Assessment for Learning*. Oxford: Oxford University Press.

20. Ibid (n 15)

21. Rosenshine, B. (2012) 'Principles of Instruction: Research Based Strategies That All Teachers Should Know', *American Educator* 36 (1) pp. 12-19.

22. Coe, R., Aloisi, C., Higgins, S. and Elliot Major, L. (2014) *What Makes Great Teaching? Review of the Underpinning Research*. The Sutton Trust.

23. Engelmann, S. and Carnine, D. (2016) *Theory of Instruction*. Eugene, OR: NIFDI Press.

24. Ibid (n 16)

25. Ibid (n 12)

26. Ibid (n 21)

27. Ibid (n 17)

28. Ibid (n 15)

HOW CAN WE DEVELOP VOCABULARY IN THE CLASSROOM?

BY ALEX QUIGLEY

Is it possible to have a thought without having words to give it meaning? Even if it is possible to hold a nameless idea in one's head, how can we express it to others until we have can give it form? Those without the power of expression are disempowered, and one of the most significant gaps between advantaged and disadvantaged children is the vocabulary gap. In this chapter, Alex Quigley looks at the importance of vocabulary teaching – not just the process of acquiring words through experience, but the business of ensuring that all of our students have a lexicon that enables them to navigate the social and intellectual landscapes of academic discourse. Vocabulary is closely linked to background knowledge, and background knowledge is essential to comprehension in different subjects. One of the most common and serious errors that teachers make is to assume what our students already know. In this chapter, Alex shares his knowledge and experience to point towards effective ways of teaching vocabulary explicitly.

Author bio-sketch:

Alex Quigley works as National Content Manager at the Education Endowment Foundation, supporting teachers and schools to engage in evidence-informed practice. Formerly, he was an English teacher and school leader for 15 years. Alex is a columnist for TES and Teach Secondary and has written books including 'Closing the Vocabulary Gap' and 'The Confident Teacher'. Alex is also a Trustee of researchED.

'Sir, what does liaise mean? And what does pulchritude mean?'

On a daily basis, every teacher navigates a wealth of questions about words and about the world. The English dictionary is replete with over half a million words and many of our pupils can struggle to stay afloat as they swim in this sea of academic language.

Given the sheer breadth and depth of vocabulary of the English language – alongside how critical it proves in mediating the academic curriculum of school – it is crucial that every teacher has a confident understanding of teaching vocabulary in the classroom. When teachers are supported to grapple with mediating the specialist academic code of school, they can gain vital answers to many of our pupils' questions. It is patently obvious that we cannot teach *all* of the words to our pupils. We know that their language develops daily, inside and outside of the school gates, with reading, talk and simply existing in the world, seeing their vocabulary grow exponentially. And yet, we can better understand how to develop our pupils' vocabulary, better identify their gaps in understanding, and to teach new words with a greater likelihood of success.

The challenge of the 'vocabulary gap'

The importance of vocabulary development to reading, writing and talk is incontrovertible. Of course, much of the vocabulary development of our pupils will happen implicitly beyond the scope of classroom instruction. This vocabulary growth is cumulative and incremental, founded upon reading and talk, and often hidden in plain sight in the busy classroom. It is the gaps in vocabulary exhibited by our pupils, rather than the subtle growth, that too often becomes clear for teachers. It manifests itself in a difficult examination, a weak answer in class or a subtly limited piece of writing.

Evidence to characterise a vocabulary gap is long-standing and sustained. A seminal study, undertaken by Hart and Risley, in America, in 1995[1] – commonly described as 'The Early Catastrophe' – is often cited as popularising the notions of the 'vocabulary gap'. It describes the meaningful differences with regards to the language experiences of young children. They estimated that before US children ever got to school, there could be a difference of language experience for children from 'word rich' or 'word poor' families, with those children from word rich families potentially hearing 30,000,000 more words than their 'word poor' peers.

The vocabulary research undertaken by Hart and Risley has rightly been critiqued.[2,3] It was a small study of only 42 families, with strong judgments being made about social class and language experience that are contestable. Their estimates, based on limited recording technology, were not directly replicated either. Crucially, however, their seminal study triggered a wave of research in this area. Rather than 'debunking' such evidence,[4] we find a consensus that a vocabulary gap exists and that teachers need to better understand the issue.

Newer research on the early 'vocabulary gap' has since showed that the gap exists and remains enduring.[5, 6, 7] Our increased understanding of the research evidence shows that the gap may be smaller than judged by Hart and Risley, but that many children come to school with having heard millions more words and having experienced many more rich interactions with parents and caregivers. We have learnt that turn taking and dialogue is of particular importance, whether that it around the dinner table,[8] or at a day out at the zoo.[9] Rich, cumulative experiences with words at an early age matter, influencing later performance in school.[10]

Crucially, teachers have revealed that the 'vocabulary gap' can hamper their pupils in countless ways. Sometimes it is 'punch-you-in-the-face' stark. From a pupil explaining they didn't understand the word 'suspense' in a GCSE exam, to pupils crying when faced with a SATs reading paper piece on 'Dead Dodo's' that they found inscrutable.[11]

In a recent Oxford University Press teacher survey, including over 1300 teachers, it was clear that vocabulary, or the lack thereof, is a salient issue for them and their pupils. Primary school teachers reported that 49% of their Year 1 pupils did not have the vocabulary to access the school curriculum. This was repeated with secondary school teachers, with teachers stating that 43% of Year 7 pupils faced the same issue.[12]

Consider for a moment the implications of such barriers. Though there are legions of challenges for a teacher supporting their pupils in the classroom, our pupils possessing the academic language required to access the school curriculum is of critical importance.

When faced with pupils who are struggling with the demands of an academic curriculum, teachers can feel unprepared. Fundamentally, our pupils' ability to read well is inextricably linked to their vocabulary.[13] Every SATs paper or GCSE examination makes that challenge explicit. For pupils with reading difficulties,[14] vocabulary instruction can be a great help, but it can be beneficial to mediate the language of school for *every* pupil.

The academic vocabulary of school

So, what makes the language of school unique? Can we describe what makes such language 'academic'?

The academic language of school is unlike the words that we use in our talk with friends and family. In school, this is evident in most of the academic reading talks, but particularly with our reading of dense informational texts (so prominent in the secondary school curriculum), we are exposed to many more rare words than in our typical talk. Indeed, if I was to read an apt story to my eight-year-old son this evening, the book we would read would likely have 50% more rare words than that of the typical professional dialogue between teachers.[15]

Researchers William Nagy and Dianna Townsend have helpfully described six common features that describe typical academic language:[16]

1. A high proportion of Latin and Greek vocabulary.
2. A high proportion of complex words that have complex spellings.
3. A high proportion of nouns, adjectives and prepositions.
4. A high proportion of expanded noun phrases and nominalisation.
5. A high degree of informational density, i.e. few words that carry lots of meanings.
6. A high degree of abstraction, i.e. words that are removed from the concrete here and now.

One of the defining characteristics of the 'academic code' of school – both in spoken and written language – is the sophisticated word choices that pack knowledge and meaning into singular words.

A grammatical term for this process – more specifically when we change verbs into nouns – is called 'nominalisation'. Put simply, it describes how when a pupil uses the verb 'sweat', we transform the words into a sophisticated noun, such as 'perspiration'. Suddenly, when our pupils deploy nominalisation in their talk and writing they begin to sound 'academic'. It makes for language that is precise, accurate and proves invariably impressive.

Many academic words in the English language are 'polysemous' (estimated to be around 70%[17]), which is to say that they have multiple meanings. This often trips up our word poor pupils.

Take the word *'prime'*. Ask your class what they think of when they hear the word prime and they'll likely mention Amazon or Optimus Prime of Transformers fame. And yet, ask every mathematics teacher and they will relate the mathematical meaning of a prime number. Even then, ask an English teacher, or a technology teacher, and they'll give the common meaning of 'first importance'. Crucially then, we need to make sure every student knows what prime means in every subject – not just mathematics.

Science in particular can prove tricky for our pupils.[18] So many words in science challenge them because their general meaning simply doesn't match their specific scientific meaning. Take 'force' in science. In the physics classroom, it has very specific and plays an important role, but then 'force' in English, history or sociology – the more general usage – can have very different connotations. As it is so central to physics understanding, teachers typically invest time in helping pupils understand the difference, but it still requires close attention.

Mathematics is a subject that is beset by a similar problem. With specialist mathematical vocabulary, such as 'acute', 'constant', 'expand', 'expression', 'factor', 'rational' and 'translation', pupils bring their common, everyday knowledge to them. Unfortunately, such partial knowledge can lead to over-confidence and pupils possessing unhelpful misconceptions. Polysemous words like 'acute' reveal the critical importance of our pupils not just knowing many words, but to know them deeply.

The magic of morphology
How do you teach a new word?

Seldom will a word be understood and used by pupils if they only ever experience that word in a long list. No word list will encompass the range of academic vocabulary – including the complex interrelatedness of such words and phrases – required by our pupils to access the entire span of the school curriculum. Instead, we must consider a range of approaches to teaching vocabulary, so that our pupils can use such strategies independently.

A common myth is that pupils need only a dictionary and access to the language of school is theirs. Consider for a moment: just how much knowledge is required to use a dictionary successfully? Pupils need spelling (orthographic) knowledge and they need to have enough depth of word knowledge to select the right word meaning when multiple options are typically offered. Dictionaries can prove a catch-22 for too many pupils.

Instead of relying on the dictionary, we can instead foreground the power of vocabulary study and developing 'word consciousness' in our pupils. That is to say, an innate curiosity to question words, to explore their roots and parts, layers of meaning, their relationships with other words (e.g. synonyms and antonyms) and so on.

A useful approach to fostering word consciousness is to explicitly teach word parts (morphology) and word histories (etymology). Human beings are pattern making machines and with language we are no different. With meanings hidden in plain sight, pupils will be breaking challenging new words into their constituent parts – what linguists call morphemes. For example, words like 'dyslexia' get broken down into the prefix 'dys' (meaning 'bad') and 'lexia' (meaning word) – being bad with words.

Rather than leaving pupils to do this haphazardly, we can harness this pattern making urge to help them better understand many of the fancy academic words that adorn our subject domains. In English literature, for example, if an author is using 'foreshadowing' then they are literally offering shadowy hints (be)'fore' something bad is going to happen in the story. These simple mental hooks add memorable meaning to words.

Take the word **'intractable'**, meaning 'hard to control or deal with'. In a history lesson this could describe Anglo/French relations during the 'Hundred Years' War', or the problems with natural resources in geography. If we dig into those mighty morphemes again then we realise something very familiar. The root of the word 'tract' – means 'to pull' – just like a tractor, with the 'in' prefix meaning 'not'. Quite literally then, the word represents how something is hard to pull apart.

The utility of teaching morphology explicitly across the school curriculum is high. We know that such knowledge is intimately related to reading comprehension success.[19] Not only that, a significant number of academic words we use in school have ancient Latin and Greek origins,[20] with the proportion being as high as 90% in areas of the curriculum like maths and science.[21]

We can see how the Latinate vocabulary of school typically makes for bigger, more complex words that we expect pupils to use in their school writing in particular:

Anglo-Saxon origins	Latin and Greek origins
Ask	Interrogate
Begin	Commence
Belly	Abdomen
Nightly	Nocturnal

(Table adapted from *Closing the Vocabulary Gap*, p. 58)

Though such words with Latin and Greek roots may be more sophisticated, and often separate from the daily language of our pupils, it offers us strategies to help pupils hook their knowledge onto new words. For example, you can study the vocabulary of religious education, and such associated worldly knowledge, and explicitly teach the morphology and etymology of singular words to open up a world of faith that can be alien to them.

Take the very word 'theology' and 'theism' that are at the very root of understanding religions. The root of the word '*theism*' is the Greek word '*theos*', meaning 'god'. The root '*the*' is at the heart of so many related terms: atheism, monotheism, polytheism, pantheism, Judaism, theology, theocracy and more.

By securing these linguistic roots, the very roots of religious understanding are unveiled to our students. Not only that, pupils begin to note that the suffix 'ology' is very common in school (meaning 'the study of…'). Patterns hidden in the English language become visible and such knowledge is compelling.

Happily, by approaching the development of the vocabulary of our pupils in this way you help pupils to not just learn one word at a time, but to learn ten.[22] They become word conscious that words have histories, parts, rich families and countless meaningful connections that open up a world of powerful knowledge.

Practical teaching strategies

How we can develop vocabulary in our classrooms can occur in countless ways. There is no singular methodology or silver bullet that emerges from the research evidence. Instead, we need to attend to developing our teacher knowledge of the challenge, whilst reflecting carefully and monitoring our approaches to explicit vocabulary instruction. We also need to carefully tend to the implicit development of language gained from reading and rich, structured talk.

Some daily strategies may include:

- **Word generation.** One approach to teaching morphology is to get pupils to generate as many words as they can from a word root or prefix. For example, the prefix 'dec' is familiar enough in words like 'decade' and 'decathlon' (from the Latin – 'decimas' – meaning 'tenth'). See how many words pupils generate in groups, then try the whole class.

- **'Word mapping'.** Our students are familiar with using graphic organisers in all sorts of guises, from Venn diagrams to Fishbone diagrams. They help translate tricky vocabulary and hard concepts into visuals models that aid understanding. For example, with 'geothermic processes' as a head word in geography, this would be followed by 'endogenic' and 'exogenic' processes. Each of these word headings then connects conceptually to other related words and processes. It is simple stuff, but it brings coherence and clarity with regard to subject specific words and ideas.

- **'Working Word Walls'.** A 'working word wall' is so much more than a display – though it may not even look very aesthetically pleasing – it is wall space that is used to recognise and record for our pupils a wealth of words. We can record new words we use in our teaching and use the wall space to highlight word roots, connect to word families, and more.

- **'Vocabulary 7-up'.** This is a simple vocabulary game that encourages pupils to record as many synonyms as they can for common words (seven ideally). So, given 'positive', 'effective', 'large' or 'small', our students exercise their capacity to draw upon a range of synonyms for those words. This activity assesses their breadth of vocabulary, but also overtly signals to students the necessary variety of words required in their academic expression.

- **'Six degrees of separation'.** The simple idea of this game is that all living things in the world are connected by six or fewer steps. Take the following vocabulary links between 'abnormal' and 'supercilious'. Straight away, pupils need to draw upon their vocabulary knowledge – of synonyms, antonyms and more – before then drawing upon their personal vocabulary knowledge. My effort? **Abnormal > strange > mysterious > special > superior > supercilious.** With a little self-explanation, you can encourage pupils to elaborate on their ideas.

Vocabulary instruction must always prove more than singling out subject specific words, compiling word lists and weekly tests. It is a fundamental part of how we communicate the vast array of knowledge at the heart of the school curriculum, not a one-off strategy.

It is helpful to leave the final word on vocabulary development to one of the most heralded researchers of the English Language: Professor David Crystal. He poses the value – the related challenges – and potential rewards of effective vocabulary instruction on offer for every teacher:

'Education is the process of preparing us for the big world, and the big world has big words. The more big words I know, the better I will survive in it. Because there are hundreds of thousands of big words in English, I cannot learn them all. But this doesn't mean that I shouldn't try to learn some.'[23]

References

1. Hart, B. and Risley, T. R. (1995) *Meaningful differences in the everyday experience of young American children.* Baltimore, MD: Paul H Brookes Publishing.

2. Sperry, D. D., Sperry, L. L. and Miller, P. J. (2018) 'Re-examining the verbal environments of children from different socioeconomic backgrounds', *Journal of Child Development* 90 (4) pp. 1303-1318.

3. Kuchirko, Y. (2017) 'On differences and deficits: A critique of the theoretical and methodological underpinnings of the word gap', *Journal of Early Childhood Literacy.*

4. Willingham, D. (2018) 'The "Debunking" of Hart & Risley and How We Use Science', *Daniel Willingham – Science & Education* [Blog], 3 June. Retrieved from: www.bit.ly/2n02290

5. Gilkerson, J., Richards, J. A., Warren, S. F., Montgomery, J. K., Greenwood, C. R., Kimbrough Oller, D., Hansen, J. H. L. and Paul, T. D. (2017) 'Mapping the early language environment using all-day recordings and automated analysis', *American Journal of Speak Language Pathology* 26 (2) pp. 248-265.

6. Huttenlocker, J., Waterfall, H., Vasilyeva, M., Vevea, J. and Hedges, L. V. (2010) 'Sources of variability in children's language growth', *Cognitive Psychology* 61 (4) pp. 343-365.

7. Rowe, M. L. (2008) 'Child-directed speech: relation to socio-economic status, knowledge of child development and child vocabulary skill', *Journal of Child Language* 35 (1) pp. 185-205.

8. Snow, C. E. and Beals, D. E. (2006) 'Mealtime talk that supports literacy development', *New directions in Child and Adolescent Development* 111 pp. 51 -66.

9. Montag, J. L., Jones, M. N. and Smith, L. B. (2018) 'Quantity and Diversity: Stimulating Early Word Learning Environments', *Cognitive Science: A Multidisciplinary Journal* 42 (2) pp. 375-412.

10. Spencer, S., Clegg, J., Stackhouse, J. and Rush, R. (2017) 'Contribution of spoken language and socio-economic background to adolescents educational achievement at aged 16 years', *International Journal of Language and Communication Disorders* 47 (3) pp. 274-24.

11. Ward, H. (2016) 'SATs: pupils in tears after sitting 'incredibly difficult' reading test', *TES* [Online], 9 May. Retrieved from: www.bit.ly/2mVn1cW

12. Oxford University Press (2018) *Oxford Language Thought Leadership Report.* Oxford: Oxford University Press.

13. Ouellette, G. P. (2006) 'What's meaning got to do with it: the role of vocabulary in word reading and reading comprehension', *Journal of Educational Psychology* 98 (3) pp. 554-566.

14. Elleman, A., Linda, E., Morphy, P. and Compton, D. (2009) 'The Impact of Vocabulary Instruction on passage level comprehension of school-age children: A Meta-analysis', *Journal of Educational Effectiveness* 2 (1) pp. 1-44.

15. Cunningham, A. E. and Stanovich, K. E. (1998) 'What reading does for the mind', *American Educator* 22 (1-2) pp. 8-15.

16. Nagy, W. and Townsend, D. (2012) 'Words as tools: Learning academic vocabulary as language acquisition', *Reading Research Quarterly* 47 (1) pp. 91-108.

17. Tennant, W. (2015) *Understanding reading comprehension: processes and practices.* London: Sage Publications.

18. Montgomery, S. L. (1996) *The scientific voice.* New York, NY: Guilford Press.

19. Deacon, S. H. and Kirby, J. (2004) 'Morphological awareness: just 'more phonological'? The roles of morphological and phonological awareness in reading development', *Applied psycholinguistics* 25 (2) pp. 223-238.

20. Nagy, W. and Townsend, D. (2012) 'Words as Tools: Learning Academic Vocabulary as Language Acquisition', *Reading Research Quarterly* 47 (1) pp. 91-108.

21. Green, T. (2008) *The Greek & Latin Roots of English* (fourth edition). Lanham, MD: Rowman and Littlefield.

22. Templeton, S. (2012) 'Teaching and learning morphology: a reflection on generative vocabulary instruction', *Journal of Education* 192 (2/3) pp. 101-107.

23. Crystal, D. (2007) *Words, Words, Words.* Oxford: Oxford University Press, p. 124.

EFFECTIVE LITERACY INTERVENTION AT SECONDARY SCHOOL

BY DIANNE MURPHY

For far too long, schools have oversimplified the problem of those children who struggle to read or write effectively. They have either assigned them labels – 'dyslexic', 'dyspraxic', specific learning difficulties' – or consigned them to bottom sets, and the corrosive effects of low expectations combined with a truncated curriculum. In this chapter, Dianne Murphy argues that the most serious learning problems require the highest levels of pedagogical skills. Interventions themselves need to be designed for maximum impact in the shortest time, and should be carefully targeted to those who need the most help. She also argues that the effectiveness of interventions is highly dependent on school leaders setting up the conditions for success. While traditionally, senior leaders have devolved responsibility for interventions to ever more junior staff, this chapter is all about what senior leaders need to know, and do, in order to ensure that all our students develop competency in the conventions of our written language.

Author bio-sketch:

Dianne Murphy is a specialist reading intervention designer. With a background in teaching, special education and linguistics, she developed Thinking Reading, a high-impact intervention specifically designed to meet the needs of adolescent struggling readers. After setting up literacy centres in New Zealand and UK secondary schools, where students achieved remarkable progress, she went on to work full-time sharing and replicating the programme in UK schools. She is a Teach First Innovation Award winner and Innovation Partner. She is co-author of *Thinking Reading: What every secondary teacher needs to know about reading.*

This chapter is divided into three main sections:

1. School context: what are the features of schools that help to ensure successful intervention?
2. What needs to be taught in literacy interventions at secondary school.
3. How interventions are best delivered at secondary school.

School context

Prerequisites to effective intervention

Too often, we see interventions as separate from school culture and systems. We expect interventions to just 'plug in' to our current way of doing things and 'add value'. But it cannot be emphasised enough that unless certain prerequisites are in place, interventions will have limited, if any, effect. The three main areas that schools need to consider are behaviour, leadership and systems.

Behaviour

Where poor behaviour is tolerated, or inadvertently condoned by inconsistency amongst staff, it is very difficult to achieve learning gains. This is because weak boundaries allow students to avoid work they find challenging or unpleasant – often through disruption or disengagement. When a culture of avoidance and disengagement is in place, students will resist and even challenge interventions – if they attend at all. Even if they do engage with an intervention, negative influences in the rest of school life can limit the extent to which gains are generalised into other areas. So, secure standards of behaviour are integral to the success of interventions.

Leadership

School leaders must have a clear vision for their school community. In practice, this means a sense of purpose: what is the school for, and what kind of pupils will it produce by the end of their schooling? Secondly, they need to communicate a sense of mission to their staff – a sense of how this mission is going to be achieved, and the part that each member of the school community will play in achieving it. This is particularly true of literacy. Ensuring that every student leaves school able to read and write properly is a moral responsibility that most teachers will support readily, if given the opportunity.

Systems

Schools need sound, pro-active systems for identifying students with problems at the earliest opportunity. These systems should be as objective as possible, and applied to all students, since many students with literacy problems have become experts at masking their difficulties. It is essential that no one 'falls through the cracks'. Schools also need systems to facilitate the timetabling of interventions, ensuring that students attend for the frequency and duration necessary to make significant gains. Lastly, schools need to have systems in place for tracking the impact that interventions are having on each student, so that staff can intervene quickly when a problem arises such as when progress begins to plateau. There is little we can do for a student if we only pick up at the very end of the programme that they weren't making sufficient progress.

The importance of screening

Interventions are not effective unless they are built on a reliable, objective system for screening students to identify those with genuine (not just apparent) literacy needs. Otherwise, some students will be allocated to intervention because they were referred by a 'squeaky wheel' teacher, while others, who may need more help, are ignored. Screening systems should not be reliant on a teacher's 'professional judgment' (i.e. 'hunch') or on how willing various teachers are to refer their students. Screening systems also need to become increasingly detailed as they identify students with more serious needs.

What should effective literacy interventions cover?

Jeanne Chall, the eminent reading researcher, distinguished 'learning to read' in the earlier years of primary education from 'reading to learn' for the years following.[1] This distinction is widely accepted[2, 3, 4] and is crucial to designing instruction for students in these later years of education. In addition to phonic knowledge, the demands of subject learning at secondary school require specific knowledge in order to facilitate comprehension, specific vocabulary to mediate domain-specific knowledge, and fluency in order to assimilate content and develop more complex academic skills.

These additional demands do not make phonics any less important. Phonics – how the written code represents the spoken code of English – is an essential foundation for understanding what is on the page. The problems caused by the guessing strategies of whole language, which seek to substitute inference from context for actual decoding skills, are well documented elsewhere.[5] Suffice to say that 20% of those arriving at secondary have been failed by insufficient teaching and need help to catch up fast. Some of that help will involve repairing a lack of phonics knowledge, but along with that deficit, other deficits in comprehension, vocabulary and general knowledge have followed and accumulated – the so-called 'Matthew effect'.[2]

The strands of reading

Boardman et al. (2008), in their excellent overview 'Effective instruction for adolescent struggling readers: a practice brief', identify six main areas for reading intervention with older students:

- Phonics (where indicated)
- Comprehension
- Vocabulary
- Word study
- Fluency
- Motivation

In addition, they point out that careful, close assessment is a crucial prerequisite for effective teaching of reading.[6] What follows is a brief overview of the six areas above.

Phonic knowledge

There is a group of students, some of whom will also exhibit comprehension difficulties, who have significant gaps in their phonic knowledge. Screening systems should identify these students as early as possible. Despite the fact that they will likely possess their own idiosyncratic learning histories[6] (and are therefore likely to need one-to-one instruction), they all need to master the same body of knowledge.[7] Not all phonics programmes are suitable or effective: many are designed for early readers. Age-appropriate subjects and language are very important when working with adolescents. Intervention teachers will need to be highly conversant with the body of phonics knowledge, or else they will need access to a programme that provides a systematic, explicit approach to explaining it. (Note: Secondary colleagues often assume that all primary teachers are experts in phonics. This not necessarily the case.)

Comprehension

Whether the focus of the programme is decoding, comprehension, or both, the student must have the opportunity to demonstrate their understanding of what they have read. It is also essential that the teacher knows whether or not the student has understood, so that appropriate remedial action can be taken if necessary. For example, where students have improved their decoding knowledge and are fluent at their grade level, but have difficulties in comprehension, they can be allocated to a comprehension strategy intervention. Such instruction can be very effective over a relatively short time[8] and will support classroom work on background knowledge and vocabulary. However, it can never be a substitute for the background knowledge which needs to be taught in each subject.

Vocabulary

Vocabulary building is an ongoing process which can be richly and successfully pursued in the regular classroom. During intervention, however, there is the opportunity to link vocabulary closely with spelling and word study, and to the close study of an appropriate portion of written text. Given that intervention time is likely to be limited, the focus for vocabulary teaching should be to ensure that students gain the knowledge they need to access the text that they are currently studying in the programme. There is, of course, also the possibility of setting additional independent work for students to develop independent reading and word-learning habits. Vocabulary-only interventions are unnecessary, as word knowledge needs to be built in the context of developing background knowledge. (See Alex Quigley's chapter on explicit vocabulary teaching for more detail on this topic.)

Background knowledge

Intervention should broaden rather than restrict students' knowledge of the world. Reading a range of fiction and non-fiction texts at the student's current level, and ensuring that decoding skills and vocabulary knowledge are taught so that the student can extract meaning from the page, enables them to experience – often for the first time – the sense of empowerment and pleasure that comes from learning through reading. Using a range of texts about different domains – geography, astronomy, history, and biology, for example – is an opportunity to develop students' knowledge of the world. As this is one of the main goals of teaching children to read, interventions should be intentionally outward-looking in terms of reading subject matter. Stimulating subject matter is also necessary as a springboard for developing students' writing skills.

Explicit language teaching

Sometimes referred to as 'word study', such instruction is designed to show students common syntactic and semantic relations between words. The study of verb inflections, prefixes, suffixes and other morphemes helps students to see that there are common patterns in English, which enable them to deduce the meanings of unknown words. The suffix '-ment', for example, implies that a verb has been transformed into a noun (government, adornment, alignment). The study of word roots can include their etymology, and the use of what Boardman et al. (2008) term 'additive instruction' to identify and link related groups of words.[9] For example, the terms 'hypothesis', 'synthesis' and 'antithesis' are all related through the root 'thesis'. (Again, see Alex Quigley's chapter on vocabulary and morphology for more details.) Making these language patterns explicit for students requires both careful programme preparation and clear teaching presentation.

Fluency

It is not enough for students to become accurate in their use of decoding knowledge. To be truly useful, this knowledge must be accessible at very high speeds. The neuroscientist Stanislas Dehaene notes that skilled readers decode and understand words at a rate of 300 per minute, that is, in about 0.2 seconds each.[10] This level of automaticity in reading is what makes it so difficult for researchers to understand the processes involved: they are happening rapidly, below the threshold of conscious awareness. What looks like 'just seeing the word' is, in fact, a very rapid linking of the sequence of symbols on the page to a sequence of sounds, identifying the word in our spoken vocabulary, understanding its meaning in context, and drawing on our experience and our knowledge of its usage to determine connotations or inferences. That is a lot to do in 0.2 seconds!

For students' gains in interventions to be long-term, it is crucial that students maintain very high levels of fluency, in order to, firstly, establish the word and its associations in long-term memory and, secondly, free up short-term working memory to focus on comprehension. Not only does fluency ensure that gains from interventions can be maintained, it can also 'eliminate so-called learning disabilities that were previously considered irremediable'.[11]

Two further domains essential for the mastery of literacy conventions are spelling and handwriting.

Spelling

Spelling is often treated as a rote exercise that is best approached by practising lists of words. As Rhona Stainthorp's chapter on spelling shows, there are multiple strategies for how proficient spellers learn to spell new words. Spelling can be taught as a reversal of the process of reading. Moats et al. (2008) argue in 'How words cast their spell' that 'effective spelling instruction explicitly teaches students sound-spelling patterns. Students are taught to think about language, allowing them to learn how to spell – not just memorise words […]. As a result, linguistically explicit spelling instruction improves spelling of studied words and novel words.'[12]

Handwriting

Once they reach secondary school, and often long before this, students cease to receive corrective feedback on their handwriting. However, handwriting is integral to students' engagement with written language in much the same way as reading.[13] Even small amounts of handwriting can generate regular specific feedback from the teacher; over time this feedback can make a significant difference to students' performance.

How to best deliver interventions: teaching, timing and structure

Detailed assessment

We have already touched on the importance of assessment for identification earlier in the book. While there is a general concern in education about over-testing of students, we are not concerned here with high-stakes testing or group ranking. Rather, we are concerned first with accurate identification of those in need of intervention, and secondly with ensuring that we have accurate information that will enable us to plan sharply targeted teaching. We need to find out exactly where students' knowledge gaps are, and ensure that these are filled. We need to make sure that we are not teaching material that the student already knows. We need to understand their levels of fluency and build these up to a practically useful level, both for long-term memory and for combining with other skills. And, as has been stated earlier, we need to know the domains of difficulty – decoding, comprehension, and/or motivation. Effective intervention will always rest on detailed assessment information, at the text, word and sound-spelling levels.

Teach to fluency

One of the main blockages to progress is not that children fail to learn when they are initially taught, but that they do not receive sufficient practice to become fluent in those same skills. Too often in education we think we have achieved our goal for students when they have become accurate, but actually, until students are fluent, they have not mastered the material. Another reason for entrenched difficulties is that students may have failed to acquire basic information, not because they were incapable of learning but because the presentation of the material was (to the student) ambiguous or confusing. It has long been known (but rarely discussed in teacher training) that we learn in a hierarchy of stages.[14] The key teacher actions required at each stage of learning are:

- **Acquisition:** Unambiguous presentation with guided practice and immediate feedback.
- **Accuracy:** Continued, spaced practice with a high accuracy criterion (usually 80-100%).
- **Fluency:** Daily timed practice with carefully sequenced practice materials to a high rate per minute.

- **Retention:** Scheduled review of previously learnt materials (spaced retrieval).
- **Generalisation:** Practice in adapted contexts or in combining the target skills with other previously learnt skills.
- **Adaptation:** Opportunities for independent, creative problem solving.

Effective intervention will make provision for addressing all of the first five stages. The final stage is more likely to be useful for extension work in the general classroom, or independent study.

Attention to sub-skills or 'tool' skills

Integral to the stages of learning model is the assertion that the skills we perform on a regular basis, even those that we think of as basic, are in fact made up of many component skills.[15] For example, walking requires coordination between the eyes and the limbs, coordination between arms and legs, proprioception (balance and orientation) and decision-making about direction and speed. When we break it down to this level, even tying a bow knot on a shoe is remarkably complex. When it comes to reading, the sub-skills are many and varied, and a lack of accuracy or fluency in any one can lead to difficulties. Effective assessment will be designed so that weaknesses in sub-skills can be rapidly identified and addressed. For example, we can check the student's fluency at reading oral prose and provide fluency practice to build this up if they do not meet the minimum fluency criterion.

An enormous body of work has been collected on the fluency criteria students need to achieve in order for teachers to be confident of effective retention, and of successful combination with other skills. For example, Kubina (2002) provides an extensive list of fluency criteria for a wide range of tool skills.[16] Johnson and Layng's classic 1992 paper, 'Breaking the structuralist barrier: literacy and numeracy with fluency', gives some striking examples of the power of fluency to enable 'curriculum leaps'.

> Haughton (personal communication, August 1978) found that college students having trouble in calculus could improve their performance by building fluency on very basic elements, such as saying and writing numbers and math facts. Haughton (1971, 1972, 1980) reported that a program of tool skill building improved underachieving students' math performance to the level of their competent peers, whereas an arbitrary reward system, increasing the potency of consequences, and extensive practice in math at the students' grade levels all failed to improve their performance. Again, the presenting problem is not always the problem to solve.

Progress in complex tasks depends on high prerequisite skill performance. Our charts show us again and again that the higher the prerequisite skill rates, the faster a complex skill will be learnt.[17]

Carefully calibrated steps in learning

There is another barrier to learning that students frequently encounter: the steps in the curriculum are too large – often because students lack the fluency in the tool skills that teachers assume they possess. However, the difficulties associated with negotiating large steps in learning are particularly punishing for students with weak reading who are already struggling to keep up and whose motivation is suffering as a result. Effective intervention requires careful calibration of content to ensure that each new step is achievable. This is consistent with Engelmann and Colvin's assertion regarding Direct Instruction programmes: 'The amount of new information presented must be small enough that mastery could probably be induced in a few minutes.'[18] Planning to this level of detail is frequently absent from intervention programmes, many of which are presented as a resource for teachers rather than a carefully controlled procedure. The result is that students continue to struggle, and their learning problems remain unresolved. The level of detail to which the teaching material must be analysed by the programme designer is frequently underestimated.[7]

Scheduling of programme components

We have looked at many of the components of effective intervention. However, some research indicates that the ways in which these components are arranged in an intervention can have a considerable impact on the students participating in the programme:

> Outcomes showed clearly that modality of instruction can matter considerably for these older struggling readers. The differences in gains clearly demonstrate that the additive modality, with its sequential addition of each component (isolated phonological decoding instruction, followed by addition of spelling instruction, followed by addition of fluency instruction, and finally the addition of comprehension instruction) is potentially the best modality for remediating reading skills (decoding, spelling, fluency, comprehension) in older struggling readers. ... These students show that they are highly sensitive to the scheduling of the components and the amounts of instructional time per component.[19]

Note that the sensitivity to scheduling applies to adolescent struggling readers.

Calhoon and Prescher found compelling indications that the level of improvement by their adolescent sample and the percentages of students classified as gainers were influenced by the way that elements of a common curriculum were organised and sequenced during instruction.[20]

Some of this effect appears to be related to developing tool skills to accuracy and fluency. Other elements may well be linked to motivation and students' sense of confidence and success.

Motivation

As Boardman et al. (2008) pointed out, motivation is a particular concern with struggling older readers. A long history of difficulty with reading is likely to create a sense of aversion, and has a negative impact on self-esteem and confidence. It is, therefore, essential that interventions take this into account. One way of doing this is through programme design. There is a conventional idea in teaching that lessons should open with a 'hook' to engage students. The problem with this approach is that students quickly learn that after the first five minutes, lessons rarely continue to be as interesting as they appeared at first. In behavioural terms, it is important to ensure that the first activity in the lesson is one with which the student is familiar with and, while providing an element of challenge, has a high probability of success. This gives the student an early positive experience, which is essential for those with low motivation, and often high levels of anxiety, around reading. In fact, the Premack principle[21] suggests that the most enjoyable activities should be scheduled towards the end of the lesson, so that they reward the effort that the student has made up to that point.

Another area in which programmes should take account of student motivation is the length of each phase of the lesson. Practice activities should be timed and short. New learning activities should focus on a limited set of items with highly prescriptive teacher presentation to ensure efficiency and immediate success.

A further aspect of effective motivational management is the teacher's moment-by-moment interaction with the student. Effort, concentration and progress should be recognised and commented on. Such comments should be brief, specific and contingent: 'Well done on arriving so promptly, let's get to work' or 'You concentrated really closely, good effort.' Training and coaching in such motivational styles is very important to the success of interventions, but managers who are allocating staff frequently overlook these needs. The area of motivation management is broad, complex and frequently misunderstood.

It cannot be overstated that children need effective teaching, not sympathy or disability-focused discourse that lowers expectations. Instead, teachers need training in skills like contingent reinforcement, behavioural observations, analysing behavioural contingencies, reinforcement schedules, fading, prompting, antecedent control, and effective use of feedback, to name but a selection of the possibilities.

How should we choose a literacy intervention?

There is a useful analogy here with medicine. With a health problem, we would select a treatment primarily on its suitability to address the issue we are concerned with. We would then consider ease of administration, potential risks, and financial cost. In much the same way, when considering an intervention, we need to have good information about the exact nature of students' needs, so that we know that the chosen intervention is going to be effective. To take an obvious example, if students' need is to improve their phonic knowledge, they should not be assigned to a comprehension class, and vice versa.

Secondly, we need to know that there is a reliable evidence base to support the intervention. Many programmes may be effective but do not have experimental data to support them, due to the cost of setting up and running randomised controlled trials. However, Stanovich and Stanovich (2003)[22] argue that the teaching approaches employed in a programme can be evaluated against the body of research now available. For example, one-to-one tuition has been shown to have a consistently strong effect. Likewise, fluency building activities have been shown to produce large gains. Greg Brooks' *What works for children and young people with literacy difficulties* gives useful comparisons of both published and unpublished datasets on a wide range of interventions at primary and secondary school, in reading and spelling.[23]

Here are some questions to ask when selecting an intervention:

Evidence base

- Is there a clear connection between the programme design and the recommendations of research, both for teaching and for content?
- Is there evidence of a rate of progress fast enough to close the gap between target students and their peers?

Targeting

Are there clear selection criteria for identifying that students will benefit from the programme?

Fidelity

Is there a comprehensive training programme so that staff involved in delivery are confident that they can deliver lessons as intended?

Materials

Are the materials:

- age-appropriate?
- accessible?
- challenging?
- suitable for the focus (e.g. decoding comprehension etc.)?

Curriculum design

- Is progress between lessons calibrated in small, achievable steps?
- Has the content been carefully analysed to manage potential misconceptions and confusions?

Opportunity cost

- How much time does the intervention require to have a significant impact?
- How much will this impact their access to the curriculum in affected subjects?

Generalisation of benefits

Does student learning generalise beyond the intervention? In other words, what evidence is there that it improves students' access to the curriculum?

Duration of benefits

What evidence is there that students' gains are sustained beyond the duration of the intervention? If students revert to their previous levels of performance, it is questionable whether it is creating more problems than it solves.

Summary

When implementing interventions, it is essential to ensure that the school context is aligned with the aims and methods of the intervention. In particular, senior leaders need to have a clear strategic plan for implementing an intervention plan rationally, coherently and comprehensively. Interventions should cover all literacy conventions where students need to become more accurate and more fluent. The level of sophistication required for developing such programmes is often underestimated, as is the level of teacher knowledge required to deliver such programmes effectively. Selecting an appropriate programme requires patient, thorough research judged against objective, measurable criteria. School leaders need to ensure that sufficient resources are available to deliver selected programmes with fidelity.

References

1. Chall, J. S. and Jacobs, V. A. (1983) 'Writing and reading in the elementary grades: developmental trends among low SES children', *Language Arts* 60 (5) pp. 617-626.

2. Stanovich, K. E. (1986) 'Matthew effects in reading', *Research Reading Quarterly* 21 (4) pp. 360-407.

3. Boardman, A. G., Roberts, G., Vaughn, S., Wexler, J., Murray, C. S. and Kosanovich, M. (2008) *Effective instruction for adolescent struggling readers: A practice brief.* Portsmouth, NH: RMC Research Corporation, Center on Instruction.

4. Hempenstall, K. (2013) *A history of disputes about reading instruction.* Eugene, OR: National Institute for Direct Instruction.

5. Hempenstall, K. (2002) 'The Three-Cueing System: Help or Hindrance?', *Direct Instruction News.* Eugene, OR: National Institute for Direct Instruction.

6. Boardman, A. G., Roberts, G., Vaughn, S., Wexler, J., Murray, C. S. and Kosanovich, M. (2008) *Effective instruction for adolescent struggling readers.* Florida: Centre for Instruction.

7. Moats, L. C. (1999) *Teaching reading is rocket science.* Washington, DC: American Federation of Teachers.

8. Willingham, D. T. (Winter 2006/07) 'Ask the cognitive scientist: The usefulness of brief instruction in reading comprehension strategies', *American Educator* pp. 39-50. Retrieved from: www.bit.ly/2mUPqQj

9. Roberts, G., Torgesen, J. K., Boardman, A. and Scammacca, N. (2008) 'Evidence-Based Strategies for Reading Instructionof Older Students with Learning Disabilities', *Learning Disabilities Research & Practice* 23 (2) pp. 63-69.

10. Dehaene, S. (2011) *The massive impact of literacy on the brain and its consequences for education.* Human Neuroplasticity and Education. Vatican City: Pontifical Academy of Sciences. Retrieved from: www.bit.ly/2nTvPk7

11. Binder, C. (1988) 'Precision teaching: measuring and attaining exemplary academic achievement', *Youth Policy* 10 (7) pp. 12-15.

12. Joshi, R. M., Tremain, R., Carrekere, S. and Moats. L. C. (Winter 2008/09) 'How Words Cast Their Spell', *American Educator* pp. 6-43. Retrieved from: www.bit.ly/2Jfb8Hx

13. Graham, S. (2009) 'Want to improve children's writing? Don't neglect their handwriting', *American Educator* pp. 20-40. Retrieved from: www.bit.ly/2rYkUH1

14. White, O. R. and Haring, N. G. (1980) *Exceptional teaching for exceptional children* (second edition). Columbus, OH: Merrill.

15. Johnson, K. R. and Layng, T. V. J. (1992) 'Breaking the structuralist barrier: literacy and numeracy with fluency', *American Psychologist* 47 (11) pp. 1475-1490.

16. Kubina, R. M. (2002) Performance standards (or fluency aims), *Dr Mike Beverley* [Blog], 12 March. Retrieved from: www.bit.ly/2pneC2T

17. Ibid (n 15)

18. Engelmann, S. and Colvin, G. (2006) *Rubric for Identifying Authentic Direct Instruction Programs.* Retrieved from: www.bit.ly/2oyJPj2

19. Calhoon, M. B. and Prescher, Y. (2013) 'Individual and group sensitivity to remedial reading program design: Examining reading gains across three middle school reading projects', *Reading and Writing: An Interdisciplinary Journal* 26 (4) pp. 565-592.

20. Calhoon, M. B., Scarborough, H. S. and Miller, B. (2013) 'Interventions for struggling adolescent and adult readers: instructional, learner, and situational differences', *Reading and Writing* 26 (4) pp. 489-494.

21. Cooper, J., Heron, O. and Heward, W. (2007) *Applied Behavior Analysis.* Harlow, Essex: Pearson Education p. 267.

22. Stanovich, P. J. and Stanovich, K.E. (2003) *Using research and reason in education.* Jessup, MD: National Institute for Literacy. Retrieved from: www.bit.ly/2nGPwf0

23. Brooks, G. (2016). *What works for children and young people with literacy difficulties? The effectiveness of literacy schemes* (fifth edition). Evesham, Worcestershire: Dyslexia-SpLD Trust.

CPSIA information can be obtained
at www.ICGtesting.com
Printed in the USA
LVHW081651211119
637767LV00004B/1/P